DISARMAMENT

...NUCLEAR SWORDS OR UNILATERAL PLOUGHSHARES?

DAYS OF DECISION

Series Editor: Julia Neuberger

DISARMAMENT
...NUCLEAR SWORDS OR UNILATERAL PLOUGHSHARES?

PAPERMAC

First published 1987 by
PAPERMAC
a division of Macmillan Publishers Limited
4 Little Essex Street London WC2R 3LF
and Basingstoke
Associated companies in Auckland, Delhi, Dublin, Gaborone,
Hamburg, Harare, Hong Kong, Johannesburg, Kuala Lumpur,
Lagos, Manzini, Melbourne, Mexico City, Nairobi, New York,
Singapore and Tokyo

British Library Cataloguing in Publication Data
Neuberger, Julia
    Disarmament: nuclear swords or unilateral
    ploughshares?——(Days of decision).——
    (Papermac).
    1. Disarmament
    I. Title   II. Carver, Michael Carver, *Baron*
    III. Chalfont, Alun Gwynne Jones, *Baron*   IV. Kent, Bruce   V. Series
    327.1′74   JX1974

ISBN 0-333-44768-9

Typeset by Columns of Reading
Printed by Richard Clay Plc, Bungay, Suffolk

Contents

Introduction

The intellectual debate on disarmament centres around the 'arms race' idea. There have been agonisings about the nature of the dangers for forty years and more, and, although international tension is not a modern phenomenon, the division into Eastern and Western bloc mentality has made it very much clearer.

The honest doubter has to look at five main issues with a clear mind in order to draw his or her conclusions. These are the key issues of the debate, but they are not always all addressed by the political parties in their policies. The first is the question of strategic intent – what a country or alliance is trying to achieve and how – and how that strategy is viewed by the perceived enemy. The second is the instability of crisis situations, and whether these lead to 'accidental' wars and attacks. The third is the question of technical and human malfunctioning and failure – how relevant that is to the debate is a moot point. The 'experts' refuse to take it seriously, but the ordinary layman can do nothing else, and Dr Bracken and Dr Ball and others have documented devastating inefficiency and confusion in arrangements for command and control. Professor Michael Howard argues: 'The capacity of the President of the United States to control his nuclear weapons-systems under crisis conditions is gravely in question, and there is no reason to suppose that that of the Soviet Union is any better.' The fourth view is that of proliferation of weapons and their attendant dangers, and the fifth is the cost to the economics of the powers concerned, and whether that can be justified.

In a nuclear age these questions have never been more urgent.

Julia Neuberger

Choices for Defence

Field Marshal Lord Carver

Successive administrations of opposing political views have found, when they have come to power after a general election, that they had very little room for manoeuvre when it came to defence and associated matters. Conservatives, when they have been out of office, have accused Labour administrations of neglecting defence and have promised to do much better themselves. Labour, in the same position, has promised reductions of defence expenditure in favour of social services, and an emphasis on disarmament and arms control. Both have soon found themselves up against the inexorable facts of economic and financial life: the apparently insatiable appetite for finance of all public services, central and local; the seemingly irreversible trend of defence costs, even a defence budget increasing at about 3 per cent per annum in real financial terms buying smaller and smaller forces in terms of numbers of combat units; the inescapable key position of Britain in NATO, which means that any change in our contribution, particularly one which involves a reduction in forces of any kind, sends tremors through the alliance, the cohesion and strength of which is the cornerstone of our defence; finally, Britain's economic and financial state, which is determined much more significantly by international factors than by those which can be directed or influenced by the British Government. The change from the usual pattern has arisen, first, because the Labour Party is not promising a reduction in defence expenditure, but a diversion, as far as one can make out, from naval nuclear to naval conventional; and, secondly, because there is now a joker in the pack, which has to be taken seriously, in the form of the Alliance between the Liberal and the Social Democrat parties, who have cobbled together a very reasonable policy.

Looking at the issues from the point of view of a prospective voter (and as a peer I can afford an objective view, having no vote) one must approach them on two planes: what choices do the parties offer, and what are the real choices? None of the parties offers the pacifist line: there are no votes in that. The Green parties of Europe, although they have many sympathisers in the Labour and Liberal parties, have no equivalent in Britain. The second plane inevitably involves technicalities, which are seldom, if ever, the stuff of election campaigns. As a professional soldier, albeit one of respectable vintage, I cannot but express my dismay at the way in which the real defence choices become submerged under the instant remedies which the politicians, the media, and those who profit from both, expound.

The Conservatives would have us believe that the maintenance of an independent British force, capable of delivering megaton nuclear warheads on Moscow, is the cornerstone of our defence, and that the replacement of the current system, four nuclear-powered submarines carrying the American Polaris missile to deliver a British designed and built warhead, must take priority over all other forms of defence expenditure. No other form of defence expenditure, they argue, whether on ships, aircraft, tanks or guns, would provide such an effective contribution to our defence, or indeed to NATO as a whole.

The Labour Party's defence policy is almost as far removed from that as it is possible to be: that not only should we in Britain abandon our own nuclear weapons, carried both in submarines and by various types of aircraft, but we should tell the Americans to remove their warheads and means of delivery from this country. In addition, it appears, they would insist that British forces in NATO would not man delivery systems with US warheads, and they would do their best to persuade fellow-members that the alliance should renounce reliance on nuclear weapons altogether, even as a retaliatory force to deter the Soviet Union from itself having recourse to them. In spite of taking that radical non-nuclear line, the party appears to be able to convince itself that Britain could remain a full member of the alliance, still exercising influence within it. To give that some tinge of credibility, Labour officially supports a strengthening of Britain's conventional force contribution to NATO, laying emphasis on the Navy. No very clear reasons are given for that preference. One can surmise that the possibility of it bringing employment to the ship-building industry is one; the traditional distrust of the Army by the political left, who see it as liable to be used to break strikes or suppress the workers, although far-fetched these days, may be another.

With somewhat uncertain steps, the Liberal–SDP Alliance treads a winding path in between, in danger of deviating both to an SDP-influenced right, in support of an independent nuclear deterrent, and to a Liberal-influenced left in support of a non-nuclear stance and what are known as 'alternative strategies'. Genuflecting in both directions, the Alliance's policy emphasises the European dimension, playing down the American, although recognising the vital importance of maintaining the latter's support of European defence. For a brief period immediately before the 1986 party conferences, the Alliance leaders gave their support to the concept of a European minimum deterrent, consisting of the British and French strategic nuclear strike forces which would somehow be coordinated – although the French gave no indication, as one would have expected, that they would in any way accept any diminution of the independence of theirs. It was not at all clear what the relation of the force would be to NATO.

Before any of these delicate aspects of the concept were clarified, it was rejected by the Liberal Party conference. In a subsequent meeting between representatives of the two parties, they agreed a formula, stating that they would maintain 'our minimum deterrent until it can be negotiated away as part of a global arms negotiation process, in return for worthwhile concessions by the Soviet Union which would enhance British and European security.' In modernising our deterrent, if and when that was necessary, they would freeze it 'at a level no greater than that of the Polaris system'. Their spokesmen have also made it clear that it would be assigned to NATO and not regarded as an independent strategic system. That formula provides a somewhat vague aid to navigating a course between the Scylla of the Tories' increase of nuclear capability with Trident and the Charybdis of Labour's unilateral abandonment of nuclear support to NATO's defence.

On other defence issues, the Alliance policy attempts to follow the same path. While laying emphasis on conventional forces in order to reduce NATO's reliance on nuclear weapons, it rests a pious hope on containing their cost by greater European cooperation, and on concentrating on forces and weapon systems that are 'self-evidently defensive'. In that context, its hopes are based on seeing that any addition to NATO's forces is based on the use of reserve manpower. On the controversial and difficult issue of the exploitation of high technology, the Alliance takes refuge in well-worn platitudes about the advantages to be gained from less self-reliance, greater European cooperation and standardisation, and the need to 'sort out' with 'prudence' the 'vast diversity of its applications' to weapon systems 'into an order of usefulness and priority'. Improvements in conventional forces are to be paid for from savings made by reductions in forces maintained for commitments outside NATO, including the Falklands, and by cancelling the Trident programme. The Alliance policy also lays emphasis on the need to look at defence and disarmament policies as one, contributing to the common security of all the countries of Europe, west and east of the Iron Curtain. It looks forward to a time when the Soviet Union has withdrawn its forces behind its own frontiers and those of the United States are all west of the Atlantic.

These are the choices offered by the political parties. The Conservatives: the mixture as before with a strong emphasis on Britain's own nuclear contribution and support of US nuclear policies (although, after Reykjavik, with some definite misgivings), accompanied by a hard line on public expenditure which actually involves a reduction in the defence budget of about 7 per cent in real terms. Labour: a radical antinuclear, basically anti-American policy, with very serious implications for the NATO alliance, and a pretended enthusiasm for conventional forces which is not accompanied by any clear commitment to provide the resources for supporting it. The Alliance: a sweetly reasonable policy between the two, the possibility of implementing which depends on being able to convert some pious hopes into reality.

Are these, or should they be, the real choices which face a future British government in determining its defence policy?

First, the nuclear question. President Reagan's meeting with General Secretary Gorbachev at Reykjavik has greatly confused an issue which had already been complicated by the launch of the US Strategic Defense Initiative. Until that – embellished by 'the President's vision' of 'rendering these nuclear weapons impotent and obsolete' – had been sprung on his unsuspecting allies, Europe had rested content to shelter under a nuclear umbrella, the mainstay of which was a belief in the strategic stability of a situation in which the two great Superpowers maintained a capability of wiping each other out. As long as that was the case, the risks to both of allowing their forces to engage in direct conflict with each other, and the presence of the forces of both on either side of the Iron Curtain, appeared to be a stable guarantee that the status quo in Europe would be preserved. When, on previous occasions, it had appeared that the Superpowers were about to reach agreements which would restrict the ability of the USA to deliver nuclear weapons against targets within the Soviet Union, and vice versa, while the Russians retained (and indeed with their SS20s significantly increased) their capability of delivering nuclear warheads on targets all over Western Europe, the European members of NATO, in particular the Federal Republic of Germany, had become concerned about 'decoupling'. That phrase refers to the weakening of the threat that a Warsaw Pact invasion of Western Europe could escalate to a strategic nuclear strike against the Soviet Union. This was seen as undermining the general nuclear deterrent to war, making it likely that, if a war broke out and led to a nuclear exchange, it would be limited to

Europe west of Russia; and that, short of war, it would lead to 'nuclear blackmail', in other words make it possible for the Soviet Union to intimidate the countries of Western Europe into adopting policies favourable to itself, as Hitler had done, by the threat of war.

It was these anxieties, it is reliably reported, which led to the decision to deploy US Tomahawk cruise missiles on the territory of the European members of NATO and to upgrade the Pershing Ia – the range of which from West Germany did not make possible attack on targets within the Soviet Union – by the Pershing II, which did. These two weapon systems were intended to reassure the Europeans that the threat of US attack on targets within the Soviet Union, in the event of an invasion of Western Europe, remained valid. They were therefore a psychological balance to the Soviet SS20s, although no claim was ever made that they were intended as a physical counter to them. They could not be effective in that role unless they struck first, which, apart from the political inhibitions against such action, would be of uncertain value, the SS20s being mobile.

This European, largely German, sensibility over decoupling was balanced by the reaction to deployment of these missiles of all those who objected to what they saw as a proliferation in the numbers of nuclear weapons and an increasing danger both of conflict itself and of its leading to the nuclear devastation of the Continent. The Americans can be forgiven for becoming exasperated by the ambivalence of their European allies about US nuclear support: on the one hand complaining that the US nuclear umbrella was being removed or had holes in it, and, on the other, protesting when it was strengthened. The Reykjavik summit has not only resurrected all the previous arguments on the issue, but has provided a far more radical background against which NATO, and Britain in particular, has to make decisions about nuclear weapons policy. Had it not been for Mr Gorbachev's insistence on setting strict limits on research into space-based antiballistic missile systems and President Reagan's refusal to accept them, both were apparently prepared to agree to a 50 per cent cut in strategic nuclear delivery systems, to the abolition of either *all* ballistic missiles (the US proposal) or all strategic delivery systems (the Soviet proposal), and to the withdrawal of all intermediate-range delivery systems from Europe west of the Urals, those remaining – the American in the USA itself, including Alaska, the Soviet in Siberia – being limited to 100 warheads each. The possibility that the two Super-powers might have agreed on such far-reaching reductions rang alarm bells in Europe. It looked like decoupling with a vengeance. Voices were quickly raised which, although making obeisance to the desirability of reductions, tried to link them to agreements on parity in nuclear delivery systems of shorter range and achievement of mutual and balanced reductions in conventional forces.

A rationale for the proposals has been emerging since Reykjavik in statements by spokesmen for the US Administration. The Americans now admit what some of us have been saying for some time: that nuclear weapon systems that are designed to destroy potential opponents' systems (to 'support counterforce strategies', in the jargon of the trade) have a bad influence. They provoke a fear in the potential opponent that his systems will be destroyed before he can use them, which tempts him to plan either a pre-emptive strike against the threatening system or a launch-on-warning, both clearly highly dangerous in a tense international situation; and they lead to proliferation in means of delivery and warheads, as each side seeks a superiority which would insure against the destruction of its own system while the opponent retains some of his. Counterforce strategies and the systems that support them are therefore destabilising, dangerous and the principal cause of the nuclear arms race. Recognising this at last, the US Administration seeks to pursue a two-pronged policy to remedy the situation: the creation of an antiballistic missile defence which will significantly reduce the reliance that an opponent could place on the effectiveness of a strike against fixed US land-based systems; and an agreement to abolish all strategic ballistic missile systems. In their place, the ability to retaliate strategically with nuclear weapons, in order to discourage the opponent from using them, would be provided by airborne and seaborne cruise missiles. The slower flight-time and susceptibility to defensive measures of the latter makes them unsuited to a pre-emptive strike. Even if agreement is reached to abolish ballistic missiles, a defence against them would still be developed and maintained as an insurance against cheating or a threat from a third party. In the field of intermediate-range nuclear systems, both Super-powers seem to have reached the conclusion that they cancel each other out and are therefore unnecessary – an opinion which some of us have held for some time.

The US administration states its hope that it will persuade the Soviet Union to adopt the same policy. The chances of doing so appear slender, particularly when one considers the investment the Soviet Union has made in ballistic missiles of all ranges. They are likely to view the US proposals as further attempts to exploit the American lead in technology in order to undermine the strategic nuclear strength which the Soviet Union has built up. Nevertheless Mr Gorbachev clearly has an interest in trying to reduce the high proportion of the national product of his country which is devoted to defence, and in avoiding a further escalation of the nuclear arms race which would be the outcome of measures to counter the projected American defensive system.

It is against this background that a future British govern-ment would have to decide its defence policy in general, and its nuclear one in particular: a very different background from that in which current policies were developed. As with all other issues, the legacy from the past exerts a strong influence. The principal reason for Britain's decision in the 1950s to design and manufacture its own 'atomic bombs' was to influence the United States, both in its general policy towards support of the defence of Western Europe and in how American nuclear weapons were to be targeted. Nobody can now seriously pretend that Britain's own nuclear capability has much, if any, influence on either. Various explanations have been given of the rationale for Britain to continue to design and produce nuclear warheads for the American-produced missiles of its ballistic missile submarines and nuclear bombs to be delivered by RAF or Royal Naval aircraft; and for the maintenance of four submarines as an independent strategic force: that is, one which is capable of delivering nuclear warheads on Moscow in circumstances when no other nuclear force is being used against the Soviet Union or its forces, and is maintained at a state of readiness to do so twenty-four hours a day, 365 days in the year. Two fundamentally different explanations are given by Government spokesmen. The official one* is that, although the British Government has complete faith in the support of NATO by US nuclear forces, the Soviet Union might believe that, for fear of escalation of a nuclear exchange to Soviet strategic attack on American cities, the US President might hesitate to authorise the use of American nuclear weapons in the event of a Warsaw Pact invasion of Western Europe; but, because Britain is itself in Europe, the Soviet Union could have no doubt that a British Prime Minister would authorise the use of independent British nuclear forces in that event, regardless of the consequences.

It is an odd argument, which reveals little faith in the value of US participation in NATO and is almost the very opposite of the other explanation, which has been used by the Prime Minister, and was used by her and the then Defence Secretary, Michael Heseltine, during the last general election campaign: that the Polaris force is, and Trident would be, a 'weapon of last resort'. That accords better with the terms of the agreement, made at Nassau in December 1962, by which President Kennedy authorised the sale of the Polaris missile to Britain. It stipulated that the British Polaris force would provide support to the NATO Supreme Allied Commander Europe and be targeted in accordance with his plans; to which the British Prime Minister, Macmillan, managed to add 'except where Her Majesty's Government may decide that supreme national interests are at stake.' Those stipulations

---

*'The Future United Kingdom Strategic Nuclear Deterrent Force', Defence Open Government Document 80/23, July 1980.

were reaffirmed in the exchange of letters between the British Prime Minister, Mrs Thatcher, and the American President, Jimmy Carter, in July 1980, confirming agreement on the terms of the sale of the Trident missile.* What that 'last resort' when 'supreme national interests are at stake' could be, is difficult to imagine. Speculation varies from the scenario underlying the other argument, a situation in which the US President refuses to authorise the use of nuclear weapons when the British Prime Minister thinks they should be used, to a situation in which NATO has fought and lost the war in Central Europe, and the Soviet forces are lined up on the far side of the Channel. Alternatively it is regarded as an insurance against the withdrawal of American forces from Europe and the consequent collapse of the NATO alliance. Less dramatic reasons are also given: that we might find ourselves at odds with another nation, for instance Argentina or Libya, which had developed or acquired nuclear weapons, and would be at a grave disadvantage if we had none of our own; or just that we are not, for political reasons, prepared to see France as the sole nuclear-armed nation in Europe.

The official argument is the weakest of all these. The presence of American land and air forces, stationed in West Germany and other countries of Western Europe, backed by the extensive and varied nuclear arsenal of the US Army, Air Force and Navy, poses immense risks to any Soviet military adventure west of the Iron Curtain. To suggest that, in circumstances in which the Soviet Union had decided to accept those risks, she would hold back because of the calculation that Britain would disregard the risk to herself of initiating a nuclear exchange, is to venture on the absurd. That scenario leads to a further consideration: that, in any case, it could not be in the interests of Britain alone, nor even of NATO as a whole, to initiate the use of nuclear weapons. There are several reasons for this. The first is that, on the assumption that the other side replied in kind, and that the number and type of weapons employed were more or less

*Cmnd 7979.

equivalent, NATO would suffer more in proportion than would the Warsaw Pact countries. As far as armed forces are concerned, this is so because NATO's armed forces are smaller in number: even if the Warsaw Pact forces actually engaged in the invasion were more concentrated and therefore suffered a higher proportion of casualties than the defenders, the overall forces available are much greater. NATO's forces are also more dependent on a smaller number of installations, notably ports, airfields and storage facilities, than are those of the Warsaw Pact. The same is true as far as population and national infrastructure are concerned. The countries of Western Europe, except perhaps for Spain and Portugal, are more concentrated into cities and dependent on fewer vulnerable installations and services than are those of Eastern Europe, including the Soviet Union. They would suffer more proportionately from an equivalent nuclear exchange.

But the assumption that the exchange would be equivalent is not a valid one. There are those who argue – Government ministers have done so – that one should not necessarily assume that the response would be nuclear at all. The 'demonstration shot' theory relies on the hope that the shock which the Soviet Union would receive, when it realised that NATO (or Britain alone) was after all prepared to use nuclear weapons, would persuade it to halt operations and talk peace. Some of those who lean towards that optimistic fantasy place their faith on what is called 'escalation dominance': the maintenance of a whole range of nuclear weapons and delivery systems which make it possible at every level to trump the opponent's play, as one climbs each rung of the ladder of escalation all the way up to an intercontinental megaton attack on cities.

Many possible scenarios of limited nuclear war have been conjured up. All of them are theoretically possible; but they fail on the certain fact that, whatever limitation one may place on one's own action and whatever theories one may have or guesses one may make about the opponent's response, one has no means of controlling what he does. In the light of all that the Soviet authorities have said or written, and of the operational doctrine on which they train and organise their forces, all the probabilities are that, if Britain or NATO initiated the use of nuclear weapons in however limited a fashion, their response would be much less limited; that it would certainly take the form of nuclear attack on all NATO's land-based nuclear delivery systems, but would not necessarily be thus limited. To imagine, therefore, that the ability to initiate the use of nuclear weapons compensates for a deficiency in conventional forces has been a dangerous delusion ever since, in the early 1960s, the Soviet armed forces have had the capability to answer back at every level. In circumstances, therefore, in which the US President was reluctant to initiate their use, a British Prime Minister's interest could not possibly be to use an independent British force, whatever the motive.

What then of the 'last resort' argument? If NATO's forces had already been engaged and lost, and the Russians were where the Germans were in June 1940, one has to consider two scenarios: one in which nuclear weapons have already been used, and one in which they have not. In the former case, NATO's nuclear arsenal has failed either to deter a war or to win it. If Britain's nuclear resources had not already been expended in that fruitless struggle, the chances of it succeeding in preventing further Soviet victories would be small, whatever the general state of Britain itself and of her armed forces might be in those circumstances. If, on the other hand, NATO had accepted defeat rather than initiated the use of nuclear weapons, a decision which Britain would have accepted (and the implication is that, if Soviet forces were to attempt to land in Britain itself, we would threaten to use our previously withheld force against Moscow), would that threat be credible, given the overwhelming response to it which the Soviet Union could threaten in return? Actually to implement the threat would be likely to mean the almost total destruction of the country. Neither first nor last resort use of a British independent strategic nuclear force makes much sense.

How about the insurance policy against withdrawal of American support from Europe? At first sight, it sounds prudent and sensible. Some recent American attitudes would appear to have reinforced that; but deeper reflection raises doubts. Could a Western European military alliance survive American withdrawal? It is unrealistic to suppose that the United States would be prepared to leave its own land and air forces stationed in Europe, if it could not provide them with nuclear support, unless the whole attitude of the US military establishment towards nuclear weapons underwent a total transformation. The first intimation from a US administration that it intended to withdraw its forces would provoke a major political crisis in Western Europe. The key issue would be the attitude of the Federal Republic of Germany. Any attempt by it to acquire its own nuclear weapons would provoke a major crisis in relations with the Soviet Union. The Scandinavian, Mediterranean and Iberian members of NATO would almost certainly opt for some form of neutrality. In those circumstances, could a military alliance, based on Britain, France, Germany, the Low Countries and, perhaps, Italy, survive, backed by British and French nuclear forces – a 'European minimum deterrent'? I find it difficult to believe that it could inspire the necessary political and military confidence in its members to enable them, if they had to do so, to stand up to pressure from the Soviet Union in circumstances in which the latter threatened to use armed force. If either NATO in its present form or such a limited Western European alliance could survive American withdrawal, the importance which we have attached to the American presence – and which I for one still strongly do – would have been shown to have been misapplied, and we should have no qualms about letting them off the hook now. I do not therefore believe that it is worth the money to pay the premium of a British independent strategic nuclear force for an insurance policy against American withdrawal from Europe. Nor do I think that it is worth paying it as an insurance against finding ourselves in conflict with some other, lesser nuclear power. I cannot imagine what the issue could be in which the possession by us of our own nuclear weapons would be a decisive factor. In any case, for that purpose, we would not need a force of the characteristics of Trident, designed to penetrate an antiballistic missile defence, nor would we need to have four submarines in order to ensure that at least one was fully operational at all times. Finally, I would, if necessary, be prepared to let the French be the only European nation to waste its money on independent nuclear weapon systems.

What therefore should a future British government do about its existing and future nuclear weapon policy? There is no doubt that NATO's forces in Europe need to be backed by the threat of the use of nuclear weapons for two reasons: to raise high the risks to the Warsaw Pact of any military adventure across the Iron Curtain, and to make sure that the Soviet Union cannot assume that it could employ its nuclear weapons against NATO's forces or targets in NATO countries without risk of retaliation. This has to be balanced against the undoubted fact that it would be folly for NATO to initiate their use. One cannot escape from the paradox that, if one wishes to deter war by the threat of the use of nuclear weapons, one has to appear to be prepared to use them in certain circumstances; but that, if one does so, one will almost certainly finish up worse off than if one had not. For these purposes NATO needs a retaliatory force, and there is a good deal to be said, in terms both of its effectiveness as a deterrent and as a form of reassurance to NATO's European members, especially the Federal Republic of Germany, for associating it directly with Europe.

There are two aspects to the question of who should man this retaliatory force. The arguments for it being American are that it links European defence directly with the overall deterrent which the US strategic nuclear arsenal provides, and that the Soviet Union is likely to regard with greater respect a force over which the US President has direct control than one over the use of which a divided command could be inhibited. The argument for some European contribution to manning the delivery system is that it demonstrates the unity of NATO behind its nuclear policy and associates its members with the responsibility, and in some quarters the odium, that attaches to that. Such a force should be as invulnerable as possible, so that it does not present a temptation to a pre-emptive strike nor is likely to be rendered inoperable in the early phases of an invasion by conventional forces. It should not therefore consist of what are called 'battlefield' weapons. Submarine ballistic missiles would fulfil the requirement best, and that has for long been the primary function of the US Poseidon and British Polaris missile boats assigned to the support of NATO's Supreme Allied Commander Europe. That function, however, does not demand penetration of Moscow's antiballistic missile defence, which is the argument for Trident and a MIRVed warhead, nor that at least one British submarine in the force should be operationally ready at all times. The demand that it should be a land-based system stems largely from the German view that a submarine-based one is less obviously associated with the defence of Western Europe and therefore less credible as a deterrent. If agreement between the Superpowers were to be reached on withdrawal of Soviet SS20s and US land-based cruise missiles and Pershing IIs from Europe, there is a strong case for Britain to continue its contribution to SACEUR's intermediate-range nuclear force in the form of ballistic missile submarines, but they would not need missiles and warheads of the characteristics proposed for the Trident missile submarines, nor is there any reason why the warheads need be designed and produced in Britain. As is the case for other NATO nuclear delivery systems manned by the British armed forces, they could be American under dual-key control. If that contribution were to continue, and the Americans also continued to provide intermediate-range nuclear delivery systems, submarine or aircraft based, to SACEUR, there should be no objection to the proposal to withdraw US land-based cruise missiles from Europe and not to replace the Pershing Ia. If the arguments I have put forward against reliance on shorter range nuclear delivery systems to compensate for an imbalance in conventional forces are accepted, battlefield nuclear delivery systems could also be withdrawn or converted to the delivery of conventional warheads only. The question of withdrawing them to a specified distance from the Inner German Border would not then arise.

The question that does arise is whether the reduction in NATO's nuclear arsenal which this would represent needs to be related to an equivalent reduction in the Soviet Union's nuclear capability, and, if so, whether that has to be verified. My answer is no to the first question, and therefore to the second. Provided that NATO retains an effective and credible threat to respond to any use of nuclear weapons by the Soviet forces by a nuclear attack on targets within the Soviet Union itself, it does not matter how many nuclear warheads or means of delivering them on to targets in Europe the Soviet Union chooses to maintain; and, as long as NATO's retaliatory force is not vulnerable to a pre-emptive strike or to being overrun by a conventional force attack, the fact that they have more of them with which to respond than NATO has should not leave NATO vulnerable to 'nuclear blackmail', unless NATO itself believes that to be the case. One cannot be blackmailed if one does not imagine oneself to be vulnerable.

The final question is whether or not acceptance of the proposal for a mutual withdrawal from Europe of these intermediate-range nuclear delivery systems on both sides should be conditional upon agreement on a ban on chemical weapons or a mutual and balanced reduction of conventional forces. If the arguments I have presented against being the first to use nuclear weapons, and therefore against regarding them as a substitute for conventional forces, are accepted, the number and type that either NATO or the Warsaw Pact retains is not related to the number and type of other non-nuclear weapon systems. To attempt to use the possibility of reduction in nuclear systems as a bargaining chip in negotiations on chemical and other non-nuclear forces could merely serve to obstruct agreements.

The choices that face a future British government in this field are therefore as follows. First, to continue the present policy of maintaining an independent strategic nuclear force, which is also assigned to NATO, for which Britain designs and produces her own warheads, while also producing some for delivery by aircraft. The cost of producing the four submarines equipped with the Trident missile is at present officially estimated at about £10 billion at 1986 prices, representing, over the period of their procurement, about 3 per cent of the total defence budget, or 6 per cent of the equipment part of it. As about a fifth of the latter is devoted to maintenance of existing equipment, the proportion it represents of the funds likely to be available for new equipment, if one accepts the official estimate, is about 7.6 per cent. The second choice is to abandon the independent concept, but continue to contribute to the ballistic missile submarine force assigned to NATO. This would not require a system capable of penetrating antiballistic missile defences, or need to be operational twenty-four hours a day for 365 days in the year. It would need fewer submarines with fewer and less complicated warheads, and would therefore cost significantly less. If it is thought that a fleet of less than four such submarines is not worth having, or if agreement between the Superpowers is reached to ban *all* ballistic missiles, a further choice is offered: that of contributing to SACEUR's nuclear retaliatory force in another form, perhaps cruise missiles, sea, air or land based. Whether or not we continue to contribute to that force depends on a judgement between the relative value of the force being clearly seen to be American and that of the European members of NATO sharing nuclear responsibility. If we do cease to man nuclear delivery systems or cease designing and producing our own warheads, the manner in which we set about it will be all-important. To do so out of step with NATO could have serious repercussions for the cohesion and self-confidence of the alliance. If a future government decides to move in that direction, it must be in conformity with the actions and policies of the alliance as a whole. The final choice, to opt out of agreed NATO nuclear policy, and to go even further, to refuse to allow the Americans to use facilities in this country for their nuclear forces, should be firmly rejected as irresponsible and highly damaging to the alliance on which we depend.

The choice between these options in the nuclear field should be related to the need for us to continue to make a significant contribution to NATO's conventional forces, and to the need to improve the general capability of the latter in the alliance as a whole. If, as I have maintained, nuclear weapons cannot be relied on as a substitute for conventional forces, it stands to reason that the latter should be adequate to fulfil their task, which is primarily to prevent war by ensuring that a potential opponent should not think that he could gain a possible advantage by the use of armed force. The overall deterrent to war in Europe, represented by the combination of the presence of the forces of the two Superpowers on either side of the Iron Curtain and the fact that they both have the capability to inflict terrible damage on each other, strongly reinforces the deterrent of forces on the ground, backed by air and naval forces. If those forces were patently inadequate for their task, the Soviet Union, or one of its satellites in the Warsaw Pact, might be tempted to embark on an adventure which they hoped could be completed before it led to a major conflict between the United States and the Soviet Union; and whether or not that were the origin of a war, only conventional forces in adequate strength could hope to bring under control a situation in which actual armed hostilities had broken out. As long as US land and air forces are stationed in Western Europe, NATO does not need to match man for man, tank for tank, aircraft for aircraft, all the forces which theoretically the Warsaw Pact could mobilise. Its forces have to be related to the territory which they defend and at least to the quantity and quality of the Warsaw Pact forces which could be used against it at short notice. At present they are only just adequate for that in quantity, and much of their equipment, including that of our own forces, is either already qualitatively inferior to that of the Soviet armed forces or will soon become so.

There is no lack of suggestions as to how NATO's conventional force capability could be improved. All nations have to face the inexorable fact that the cost of equipment needed to counter that of the Soviet armed forces escalates at a rate above that of inflation, and that the cost of maintaining standing forces, whether conscript or volunteer, also increases in line with improving standards of living, or expectation of them, in the society from which they are drawn. Those facts, combined with demographic trends reducing the population of military age, make it unreasonable to expect the democratically elected governments of NATO to increase the size of their standing forces, and difficult for them even to maintain them at their current strength. Military experts and commentators therefore search around for solutions, coming up with ones that are generally coloured by their own interests or personal predilections.

One argument which is frequently put forward is that we cannot afford to make a significant contribution to both NATO's maritime forces and to its land and air forces on the Continent, and that we must choose between the two, the majority of those who take this view maintaining that, as a sea-girt nation, we should choose the maritime. This navalist school cites the expense of keeping some 55,000 soldiers and 10,000 airmen, a high proportion of whom are accompanied by their families, with all the overheads which that entails, in Germany.* They suggest either that the men should not be accompanied by their families (as sailors are not when they are at sea), or that the commitment, entered into under the Brussels Treaty in 1954 to break the deadlock over the rearmament of Germany, should be reduced by a general reduction in the size of the Army or by stationing some of that committed to NATO in the United Kingdom. The chances are slender that the Army could recruit enough men, and even slenderer that it could persuade them to remain in the ranks, if service in Germany were to be unaccompanied. The second option was tried by the Labour administration in the early 1960s, when a brigade was withdrawn to England. It saved little money and caused great difficulties, not least in training. The fact remains that, for a country of 56 million people, we produce a very small army. Our contribution is regarded by our allies as a minimum and is a key one in terms of the self-

---

*There were 24,000 children in Service Children's Education Authority schools in north-west Europe in 1985.

confidence and cohesion of the alliance. The Americans must be reassured that European members are contributing their fair share, and our fellow-Europeans that we are playing a full part. The absence of the French from the military organization reinforces the importance of our contribution, and it would not be in our interests to see that of Germany become predominant, as would inevitably happen if we made a significant reduction in the forces stationed in that country.

On the other hand, it is not reasonable to suggest a significant reduction in our contribution to maritime warfare capability in the Eastern Atlantic, the North Sea or the Channel. We are more dependent on the sea, and more vulnerable to attack within it or from it, than any other NATO nation, except perhaps Norway. We are better suited historically and geographically to make such a contribution than other European members, which is important in persuading the Americans that it is worth their while and operationally sensible to support with their Navy the presence of their forces on land in Europe. A choice between a maritime and a continental commitment is not open to us. It never has been. Throughout our history it has been important to us to ensure that no potentially hostile power dominates the Continent. We have had to contribute to continental alliances to prevent that. It has usually meant providing small armies of our own, paying foreign soldiers to fight alongside them, and making financial subsidies to allies. In the twentieth century the last two methods of reducing our own Army's contribution have no longer been open to us and clearly are not now. Geography, determining our history, forces us to make a delicate judgement in the balance between the maritime and the continental commitment. We cannot give one priority over the other.

What choices are open to a future government in the field of conventional forces? First, the maritime. The argument revolves around the future requirement for surface ships. Modern methods of reconnaissance mean that it is impossible to keep their presence hidden from an enemy even in mid-ocean, and modern weapons can be accurately directed to hit them from long distances over the horizon. It therefore costs a great deal to protect them, and their own contribution to anti-submarine or even anti-surface vessel operations is becoming less important in comparison to that of both nuclear-powered submarines and shore-based long-range aircraft. Those factors lay behind John Nott's policy when he was Defence Secretary, and receive a wide measure of support. The opposition comes from those who wish to maintain a 'balanced fleet'. There is no doubt that, in conditions short of major war, there is a basic minimum of surface vessels, if foreign policy and economic interest are to be supported by the presence of the White Ensign in all those areas where it might be needed or desirable. Destroyers and frigates are suitable for this task. The generally accepted figure to meet this requirement is about fifty. The argument begins over larger vessels, of which there are now only two types: the small aircraft-carrier and the assault ship. When, in the mid-1960s, Denis Healey, as Defence Secretary, forced the admirals to face the reality that to replace the ageing fleet of aircraft-carriers was beyond the country's resources, the Navy invented the concept of a ship called a 'through-deck cruiser'. It was to combine the functions of a command ship and a carrier of anti-submarine helicopters, which the Navy had concluded were more effectively concentrated in one fairly large ship than scattered about, one by one, in a larger number of smaller ones. They also had in mind, although they kept quiet about it while Healey was around, that the Harrier vertical take-off aircraft could be operated from it, its justification being to shoot down shadowing enemy aircraft, notably the Soviet Bear long-range maritime patrol aircraft. After a long struggle, they obtained approval for the maritime version of the Harrier when Roy Mason was Defence Secretary. They proudly cite the Falklands operation as proof of their farsightedness. That campaign also justified the retention of an amphibious assault capability in the form of the aged assault ships *Intrepid* and *Fearless* and the 'Landing Ships Logistic', which, when the Navy had refused to sponsor them in the early 1960s, had originally been army vessels, but which had later been transferred to the Navy as fleet auxiliaries. *Intrepid* and *Fearless* are old and crewing them is expensive in manpower. If they are not replaced, the future of the Royal Marine Commandos, which they are designed to carry, is called into question. It is difficult to imagine a situation in which a balanced fleet, incorporating these types, would be required again. To provide against it involves a large slice of the equipment budget and absorbs a significant proportion of naval effort both in terms of money and manpower, for it is not only the cost of the ships themselves and their crews which is involved, but also all the other elements which are needed to protect them and ensure that they remain effective and afloat.

There is no doubt that the principal threat stems from the large Soviet submarine fleet; nor is there much doubt that the best counter to it is close cooperation between nuclear-powered attack submarines and aircraft, for both detection and offensive action. The argument lies in deciding the balance between shore-based long-range fixed-wing aircraft, manned by the RAF, and naval helicopters, which require a surface ship as a platform. The Navy naturally tends to place emphasis on the latter, while the RAF is not keen on increasing its commitment to maritime operations, which tends to be a monotonous task, much less glamorous than flying faster and more manoeuvrable aircraft. Nott's proposals, which favoured long-range aircraft at the expense of surface ships, were based on sound reasoning.

Suggestions for improving land forces, including our own, vary from merely updating the equipment of current forces, without changing their general pattern, to low-technology 'alternative strategies' and high-tech solutions to improve fire-power, mobility or both. The electronic revolution advances at such a pace that weapon, detection and communication systems become out of date almost as soon as they come into service. Unless they keep pace with those of the Soviet armed forces, which replace their equipment at much more frequent intervals than we can afford to do, they can be rendered inoperable by enemy electronic warfare measures. New technology, however, opens up the possibility of significantly increasing the effectiveness of fire-power without increasing the demands on manpower, provided that the new systems replace, and are not merely added to, the old. It offers the possibility of much more accurate and immediate detection of potential targets by sources which, apart from airborne early warning, do not rely on manned aircraft. It also offers the possibility of immediate transmission of that information directly to those who can launch weapons to the target and to those at command levels who must decide whether or not that target is to be attacked. Finally, technology now offers non-nuclear warheads, and missiles to deliver them accurately, fired from the ground or from aircraft, which can inflict almost as great damage on targets such as airfields, bridges, buildings and concentrations of vehicles as the nuclear warheads on which NATO plans had hitherto relied for that purpose. The great advantage of the last possibility is that there should not be the same inhibitions about using these new weapon systems as soon as hostilities have broken out, as there are bound to be about the use of nuclear weapons. A serious problem will remain, if these systems, like those they would replace, are regarded as 'dual-capable'; that is, able to use either nuclear or conventional warheads. Their purpose would largely be frustrated if the enemy were to assume that they were delivering, or about to deliver, nuclear weapons when they were not.

These new weapon systems will cost a considerable sum of money; but, if they replace the aircraft on which NATO has hitherto relied for the same reconnaissance and strike tasks, nuclear and conventional, and if battlefield nuclear systems are abolished, they should not cost more (perhaps less) than replacement of those systems, the majority of which are based on aircraft. The various suggestions made, linked to controversial concepts such as 'Air-Land Battle 2000' and 'Follow-on Forces Attack', have aroused opposition as being too offensive in nature, provoking fears in the Warsaw Pact that NATO plans are offensive. In reality they consist merely of replacing concepts based on aircraft, relying heavily on the delivery of nuclear bombs, with missiles delivering either solely non-nuclear warheads or, at least, relying much less than previously on early use of nuclear ones. No Soviet military man of any standing could seriously believe that NATO's current conventional military posture is offensive or that the adoption of these new concepts would make it so. NATO's dispositions, organization, command arrangements and logistic support facilities clearly contradict that. Soviet military doctrine, sensitive to 1941, itself stresses that the ability to take the offensive immediately is the best form of defence. The organisation and training of all their forces, nuclear and conventional, is based on that concept, which is why it is so difficult to conclude arms control agreements with the Soviets. The major problem about the conversion of NATO's forces to this high-technology approach is that, in relying on it to replace reliance on nuclear weapons, the European members could not expect that it would largely be provided by the USA, as the nuclear support has been. The Europeans would be expected to man and purchase, or themselves produce, the systems, while the savings would to a large degree accrue to the budgets of the US Departments of Defense and Energy. Whether or not NATO adopts these new systems and we participate in them, there is clear evidence that the Soviet armed forces are developing them, posing a very serious threat to fixed airfields and the aircraft which operate from them.

A different high-technology approach would concentrate effort on mobility, exploiting the helicopter, of which the French Force d'Action Rapide is an example.* Nobody doubts the value of the helicopter for reconnaissance and as a carrier of anti-armour weapons, and as a transport vehicle of limited load capacity; but that limitation, and its vulnerability and susceptibility to weather conditions and visibility, cast doubt on over-reliance on it to replace surface vehicles. Helicopter fleets are expensive to buy and operate.

At the other end of the technology scale are to be found the

---

*The most sophisticated exposition of this is to be found in Richard Simpkin's *Race to the Swift* (Brassey, 1985).

advocates of alternative strategies or territorial defence.* They claim both cheapness and lack of provocation for their solutions, which vary from conventionally organised and equipped forces based primarily on reserve manpower, like the Swedish and the Swiss, to Home Guard or guerrilla-type forces, relying on absorption and subsequent harassment tactics to deter an enemy from attempts to occupy territory, or to exhaust him if he does. These solutions should be distinguished from those which advocate a greater reliance on reserve forces, some of which would resemble the more conventionally organised, as a supplement to standing forces, whether the latter rely on conscription or voluntary recruitment. The objection to this type of force, particularly the more primitive type, is that its deterrent value is low, and that its military effect is not only uncertain but depends upon a long drawn out struggle, in the course of which the nation itself can be torn apart by internal divisions, in addition to the damage inflicted on it by the occupant. In any case, it is not a solution which can sensibly be applied to Britain. We cannot afford to wait until the enemy has landed in our islands before we attempt to do anything about it.

Although the retention of a modern army of 55,000 men on the Continent is far and away the Army's most important commitment, there are other minor ones. That of Northern Ireland remains the next greatest potential absorber of manpower and is the principal justification for the fact that the Army still retains fifty regular infantry battalions, while there are only twelve tank and twenty artillery regiments, three of the latter being air defence. Until that commitment disappears, if it ever does, there is little scope for any major change in the organisation, and therefore of the cost, of the Army.†

The scope for change and the difficult decisions about the

---

*An authoritative description is contained in *Nation in Arms*, Adam Roberts (Macmillan, 1986).

†There are also six regular Gurkha and forty Territorial Army infantry battalions. There are two field artillery and four air defence regiments in the Territorial Army, but no tank units.

future lie principally with the Royal Air Force. In 1986, 38 per cent of the defence procurement budget was devoted to air equipment, the Tornado programme absorbing a large proportion of it. The aircraft they replace were very long in the tooth, but already the replacement of the Jaguar by a European Combat Aircraft is being considered, and the recent decision to buy the American Boeing AWACS aircraft to replace the antique Shackleton will take a large share of the new equipment vote.

But new technologies are calling into question whether a piloted aircraft, with all the overheads which that entails, is the best method of carrying out many of the tasks which are now assigned to them: air defence, strike and reconnaissance missions. Air defence is a particularly difficult problem. An enemy attempting to deliver bombs onto targets in the United Kingdom is, these days, not going to enter our air space, but fire a missile carrying the warhead from anything up to 200 miles away. Apart from that, the Soviet armed forces have land-based missiles capable of delivering either nuclear or conventional warheads, and sea-based ballistic and cruise missiles, all of which could be used to attack targets in this country; but the only form of air defence which the Air Defence version of Tornado, backed by the land-based and airborne radars, provides is the ability to shoot down other aircraft. For point defence of potential targets, there can be no doubt that land-based missiles are more effective, and they are probably more effective also as an area defence, if there are enough of them. However, an air defence of the whole of the United Kingdom against air-delivered missiles, cruise and ballistic missiles of all kinds would be astronomically expensive. The difficult question to answer is whether it is worth paying the cost of an air defence, based on aircraft, which is effective only against a limited number of enemy aircraft.

As I have already suggested, modern technology is also providing methods of reconnaissance and offensive strike which can be more effective, less vulnerable and less expensive in overheads than piloted aircraft; but we should not be able to afford them, unless they replace rather than are supplementary to the latter. This poses the question as to whether or not the Army, with such systems, should not itself assume responsibility for those tasks which at present the tactical Air Force performs in its support. If that were to happen, it would pose the even more difficult question of whether a separate service was the best way of manning aircraft in support of either land or maritime operations. The trend for shore-based aircraft to assume an even greater role in maritime operations than they have in the past, reinforces the argument that the Navy should assume responsibility for their operation.

If it were decided that we should revert to the pre-1918 situation, when the Army and the Navy controlled their own air arms, there would remain the contentious question of responsibility for air defence of the United Kingdom. It is worth recalling that the two principal reasons for creating a separate service in the first instance were the difficulty of coordinating the requirements of the Army and the Navy in the field of aircraft design and procurement, and the failure of the Navy to devote sufficient effort to the Air Defence of Great Britain, which was then its responsibility. The first problem has now been solved by the existence of an integrated Procurement Executive in a centralized Ministry of Defence: as to the second, one should note that the Army's Anti-Aircraft Command played a major role in that field in World War II. The independent strategic bombing role, which the separate Royal Air Force developed, has now passed to the Navy's ballistic missile submarines. The issue is clearly a political potato of the very highest temperature; but, before a future government commits itself to a new programme of combat aircraft, it should consider that issue seriously. An alternative is to merge all three services into one; but that makes no operational sense, as the likelihood of the Army and the Navy being closely associated in the same operation becomes remote, and the unsuccessful Canadian experiment serves as a warning against such a merger.

One further contentious issue, which is bound to form part

of the election defence debate, is the attitude a future government should take to the American Strategic Defense Initiative. One thing is certain: that its views are not likely to have any significant influence on the programme one way or another: that will be determined by American domestic politics and the relationship between the United States and the Soviet Union. If all the European members of NATO were united in their views, they might exert a marginal influence. Most of them, including our own government, had misgivings about it from the start; but none of them wants to miss an opportunity to jump on the technology bandwagon. A number of factors motivate that: fear of a brain drain, or of falling even further behind the USA and Japan in the development of commercially valuable technologies, and hopes that there could be spin-offs in other fields of defence or in a less sophisticated form of anti-missile defence. Misgivings as to whether or not it is a wise course to pursue arise also from mixed motives: doubt as to whether it can ever achieve its aim, and whether that aim, which is never entirely clear, is really desirable: fear that if the Soviet Union follows the same road (as the US administration appears to wish), British and French strategic nuclear forces will be nullified; fear that instead of leading to reductions in nuclear arsenals and a more stable strategic balance it will result in the opposite; and fear that devotion of financial and other resources to it will be at the expense of conventional forces. Any future British government would be wise to maintain a cautious non-committal attitude, and wait and see how the programme develops.

There are therefore some important defence issues, the shadows of which will hang over the election and certainly cause headaches to whatever administration results from it. The sooner these are faced the better, or the armed forces will continue to shrink, step by step, their effectiveness and the value for money they represent diminishing at a greater rate.

Defence and Disarmament

Lord Chalfont

One of the primary functions of any freely elected government is to ensure the safety of its people and the survival of their political institutions. Thomas Hobbes, describing in *Leviathan* the duties of a sovereign state 'on whom the Sovereign Power is conferred by the Consent of the People assembled', argued that when men and women invest authority in a government, their sole purpose is to ensure peace and security. This involves the prevention of discord at home and hostility from abroad. The government, therefore, is entrusted with 'the Right of making Warre, and Peace with other nations, and Common-wealths; that is to say of judging when it is for the publique good, and how great forces are to be assembled, armed and payd for that end; and to levy mony upon the Subjects, to defray the expenses thereof . . .' Three centuries later, it would be difficult to improve upon Hobbes's analysis of the obligations which a government undertakes in formulating and putting into effect its defence policy.

Before doing so, however, a prudent government must construct some frame of reference. It must proceed from a set of principles and assumptions upon which it can construct intelligent policies designed to promote national security, within a stable international order. A fundamental consideration is the role of armed force in relations between nation states. Frederick the Great put it in characteristically robust, if slightly enigmatic terms. 'Diplomacy without arms,' he said, 'is like music without instruments.' Sir Michael Howard, Regius Professor of Modern History at Oxford, has expressed the matter more lucidly: 'International conflict is an ineluctable product of diversity of interests, perceptions and cultures . . . armed conflict is immanent in any international system.' In other words although war can often be avoided, or its effects mitigated by patient and realistic statesmanship, it will not be eliminated from the conduct of international affairs simply because it is demonstrably cruel and destructive. Indeed it is difficult for anyone not engaged in the business of conjuring up dream worlds to conceive of a stable international system which would not ultimately rely in some way upon the sanction of force.

o   o   o

Clearly, effective arrangements for national security must include adequate military defence against any external attack. Before this can be done, the threat of any such attack must be identified and evaluated. It seems reasonable to suggest that the principal, indeed at present the only, external threat to the integrity of the United Kingdom and the survival of its political institutions comes from the Soviet Union. It is unnecessary here to catalogue in detail the various aspects of the immense military apparatus which has been constructed by the Russians in the last twenty years. Even allowing for various differences of assessment and interpretation, it is widely agreed that the Soviet Union spends a much higher proportion of its natural resources, both gross and per capita, on its military establishment than any other major power, and that it has demonstrated on more than one occasion its readiness to use its military strength ruthlessly and effectively in pursuit of its political aims.

It is, of course, possible to argue that the massive military capability of the Soviet Union is not of itself evidence of hostile intent. There are, it is sometimes suggested, alternative explanations: historic Russian paranoia about the activities of the outside world; the predominant influence of the military establishment in the Soviet bureaucracy; or a determination to ensure that any future conflict shall not be fought on Russian soil. It is always difficult to arrive at an exact assessment of the intentions of any government, however open may be its processes of decision making, and however irresponsibly incontinent may be its press and the loyal opposition. In the case of an obsessively secretive totalitarian power, with no free press and no opposition, it is virtually impossible. In the business of threat analysis, however, intentions cannot be separated from capabilities. Indeed, it is often possible to make a valid assessment of the intentions of a potential enemy only from a close study of his military capabilities – the size, strength and shape of his armed forces, their equipment, training, strategic assumptions and tactical doctrines.

In this context it is possible to assert as a general proposition that Russian military strength is entirely disproportionate to any possible requirement for the territorial defence of the Soviet Union, especially in the light of the military capabilities of any potential invader. More specifically, careful examination of the equipment, deployment, tactical doctrines and training methods of the Soviet armed forces seems clearly to suggest an aggressive posture. For example, while the annual manoeuvres of the NATO forces in Europe are regularly based upon a battle plan involving an early withdrawal in the face of a Soviet attack, followed by a defensive battle and counter-attack, Soviet and Warsaw Pact military exercises include no such defensive phase. They are designed to train military formations in rapid advance, assault, river crossings, airborne operations ahead of the main force and the use of chemical weapons to neutralise defensive positions. It may be, of course, that this can be explained by the determination of Russians to fight on the soil of her adversaries rather than that of Mother Russia, but it would be unwise to draw too much comfort from such a theory.

Furthermore, the Soviet Union has consistently demonstrated that it is prepared to use its military capabilities aggressively in any situation in which it cannot clearly and effectively be deterred from doing so. It is sometimes argued that this expansionist tendency springs more from pragmatism and opportunism than from any strategic blueprint, and that it is part of a defensive mechanism designed to preempt and neutralise the activity of potential aggressors in the West and the Far East. Those who advance this argument apparently discount the evidence of a number of defectors and dissidents from the Soviet Union and Eastern Europe who have provided persuasive, if not entirely conclusive, evidence of the existence of a grand design for global predominance. Whether or not this is so, it is important to recognise that a confrontation exists. We are engaged with the Soviet Union in a continuing conflict of faith, of ideas and of moral values. It is a conflict between two totally irreconcilable political systems, one in which the individual exists only to serve the state, and one in which the state exists to serve the individual. These two systems might conceivably coexist in something resembling peace and stability, but there can never be compromise with the values of totalitarianism. It is entirely fanciful to suppose that in the next ten or fifteen years some miraculous transformation will occur, and that the confrontation between Soviet imperialism and the free world will cease.

The conclusion of any prudent Western government must be that the military strength of the Soviet Union, in the context of its known doctrines and policies, poses a real and growing threat to Western security. This is not necessarily the threat of a sudden assault by the Warsaw Pact forces in Europe, although such a possibility should never be discounted; it may not even be a threat of direct military action at all. The danger is of a more classical kind, deriving from the political significance of military superiority. If the Soviet Union is permitted to establish a decisive superiority in military forces, both nuclear and conventional, then the mere threat of military action, whether implicit or explicit, might be enough to ensure that it could achieve virtually unlimited political aims without the need to move a single division across a national frontier.

Some assessment of the strategic doctrines of the Soviet Union is therefore essential to the process of formulating our own defence policies. One of the principal deficiencies of a great deal of strategic analysis in the West is a persistent failure to appreciate that Russian and Western strategic doctrines are based upon entirely different assumptions, cultures and habits of mind. This truth was underlined by an authoritative Russian source in *The Penkovsky Papers*, published in 1965.

One thing must be clearly understood. If someone were to hand to an American general, an English general, and a Soviet general the same set of objective facts and scientific data, with instructions that these facts and data must be accepted as impeccable, and an analysis made and conclusions drawn on the basis of them, it is possible that the American and the Englishman would reach similar conclusions – I don't know. But the Soviet general would arrive at conclusions which would be radically different from the other two. This is because, first of all, he begins from a completely different set of basic premises and preconceived ideas, namely, the Marxian concepts of the structure of society and the course of history. Second, the logical process in his mind is totally unlike that of his Western counterparts, because he uses Marxist dialectics, whereas they will use some form of deductive reasoning. Third, a different set of moral laws governs and restricts the behaviour of the Soviet. Fourth, the Soviet general's aims will be radically different from those of the American and the Englishman.

In a great deal of Western strategic analysis, many of the elements of any rational debate about nuclear deterrence, such as the disarming strike, ballistic missile defence, selective targeting, civil defence and the modernisation of theatre nuclear weapons, are dismissed too glibly on the basis that 'no one can win a nuclear war'. Yet this view derives entirely from Western value judgements and habits of thought and finds no place in Russian military thinking. A study of the most authoritative strategic writing from the Soviet Union – that of Sokolovsky, Ivanov, Gorshkov and Kulikov among others – indicates that the concept of fighting and winning a nuclear war is at the heart of Russian military doctrine. For Soviets the only effective nuclear deterrent is one which confers upon them the option of fighting a successful nuclear war if deterrence should fail. One quotation – from Sokolovsky – is enough by way of illustration:

> . . . we conclude that the Soviet Union's Armed Forces and those of the other socialist countries must be prepared above all to wage a war where both antagonists make use of nuclear weapons. Therefore, the key task of strategic leadership and theory is to determine the correct, completely scientific solution to all the theoretical and practical questions related to the preparation and conduct of just such a war.

Just as the Soviet Union, faithful to its Marxist–Leninist principles, will employ any instrument – political, economic or military – in pursuit of its foreign policy aims, so, if it chooses the military option, will it use any weapon, 'conventional', chemical or nuclear, which it believes will enable it to prevail.

Britain, like any other advanced industrial country in the West, must therefore clearly ensure that it is able to deter the Russians from *any* course of military action that would threaten its own national security. History has so far shown no way of achieving this without the possession of the classic deterrent against military attack – an effective and credible military defence.

o   o   o

Hitherto, there has been a large measure of consensus in our society and its political establishment about how the military defence of a medium-sized industrial nation like Britain should be organised. The basic framework is collective security, based upon the assumption that an alliance of like-minded nations is able to offer a more effective defence than a number of individual states which could be picked off separately by a determined enemy. Britain has chosen therefore to maintain full membership of the North Atlantic Treaty Organization. To this alliance it makes a significant contribution, in terms of both conventional defence and nuclear deterrence. A substantial section of the European theatre of operations is defended by British Army and Royal Air Force units, while the security of the communication routes across the Atlantic is partly the responsibility of the Royal Navy. Indeed, apart from special garrisons and detachments in such places as Northern Ireland, the Falklands Islands, Hong Kong and Gibraltar, Britain's conventional forces are allocated to, and fully integrated within, the North Atlantic Treaty Organization. Although they have certain critical deficiencies of strength, deployment and equipment, they constitute an important and effective element of the conventional defences of the alliance.

They are, however, like the rest of NATO's forces in Europe, attempting to implement a defensive strategy for which they are neither organised nor equipped. A certain prescription for disaster is to base national or collective security upon a carefully constructed military strategy, and then persistently fail to provide the resources necessary to implement it. It is for this reason that the ability of NATO to implement the defensive-deterrent doctrine generally known as flexible, or graduated response, has for some time been regarded with considerable reservation by a substantial body of opinion – not only among professional planners and military commanders but also among academic strategists.

Perhaps the most articulate and authoritative advocate of more realistic approaches to the defence of Western Europe is General Bernard Rogers, Supreme Allied Commander Europe, who has raised to an almost evangelical level his campaign to exploit Western technological superiority in order to offset the numerical superiority of the Warsaw Pact and so improve the deterrent posture of NATO's defensive forces. He proceeds from an assumption that the doctrine of flexible response is entirely valid, provided that the resources necessary to implement it are clearly available. The validity of this doctrine depends upon the concept of controlled escalation, in which any attack by the Warsaw Pact forces would be met at each stage by an appropriately graduated reaction, including the use of 'battlefield' or 'tactical' nuclear weapons if it proved impossible to contain the enemy advance by conventional means. This has involved the forward deployment of a considerable number of low-yield nuclear weapons to implement the first stages of the process of escalation, and, by extension, to provide a manifest deterrent against an attack with even limited objectives.

This doctrine has always, of course, implied a readiness by NATO forces to use nuclear weapons first; and it is in this context that most of the doubts about its credibility have arisen. Many serious analysts have insisted that, as tactical or battlefield nuclear weapons are for all practical purposes under ultimate American control, their first use against a conventional attack would be extremely unlikely, since there would be no guarantee of a similarly limited Soviet response. In the language of the more trenchant critics, no president of the United States is likely to put New York or Chicago at risk to preserve the integrity of the European theatre of operations. The counter argument has been that no leader of the Soviet Union could ever be sure of this, and that the inevitable doubts about American reaction were in themselves an effective deterrent. As General Rogers insists, even with adequate conventional capabilities, NATO could never be certain of defeating a conventional attack without escalation; removing the element of uncertainty from the mind of a potential aggressor by declaring a 'no first-use' policy would therefore seriously weaken the nuclear deterrent.

The Warsaw Pact, however, has always been able to outrange NATO's 'battlefield' nuclear weapons with its conventional artillery. As Dr Manfred Worner, Defence Minister of the Federal Republic of Germany, pointed out in May 1982, 60 per cent of the US nuclear weapons in Europe have a range of less than thirty kilometres and the great majority of these weapons have a range of under fifteen kilometres. 'This means nothing more and nothing less than that the greater range of Soviet tube and rocket artillery presents the opportunity for the Warsaw Pact, under many battle conditions, to destroy by conventional means NATO's nuclear insertion capability, while its own weapons are beyond the effective range of NATO forces.' The equation has been further complicated by significant improvements in the nuclear capability of the Soviet Union. The strategy of flexible response was developed over a period of fifteen years during which the United States possessed a clear degree of nuclear superiority. It was estimated in 1952 that the conventional defence of Western Europe required force levels of ninety-six divisions and 9000 aircraft to pose a credible response to the powerful ground forces of the Warsaw Pact. In the political and economic climate of post-war Europe these levels (the so-called 'Lisbon Goals') were clearly unrealistic, and even a compromise plan for fifty divisions and 4000 aircraft had no prospect of being achieved.

By 1956 NATO had decided to settle for twenty-six divisions and 1400 aircraft. These demonstrably inadequate conventional forces were to act as a 'trip wire', designed to trigger off US nuclear retaliation against nuclear attack. It was planned to deploy 15,000 'tactical' nuclear weapons which were to be, in effect, an extension of conventional fire-power. It was still the strategic superiority of the United States which was to provide a nuclear umbrella of extended deterrence for Western Europe. In the event only 7000 battlefield nuclear weapons were deployed, and in 1967 NATO adopted its strategy of flexible response, which postulated a significant improvement in conventional forces – an improvement which never materialised. Theory and fact therefore failed to coincide. There was, in fact, no capacity for flexible response: the security of Western Europe continued to rely upon a form of massive retaliation, which, so far as it has ever made sense at all, has done so only in the context of decisive American nuclear superiority.

In the meantime, that superiority has virtually disappeared. As Sam Nunn, the US Senator from Georgia, pointed out in 1982 in the course of his testimony to the Senate Armed Services Committee: 'By attaining strategic nuclear parity with the United States, the Soviet Union has severely undermined the credibility of US strategic nuclear forces as a deterrent to a conventional attack on Europe.' It is not too extreme to suggest that a strategy of flexible response, if it is widely perceived to be incapable of implementation, carries with it dangers which might eventually threaten the disintegration of the Western alliance. So long as NATO relies upon defensive resources which allow virtually no flexibility and no range of options between retreat and nuclear retaliation (between 'suicide and surrender') there is a very real danger that, in a crisis, the West might be forced to submit to military blackmail; and the growing public awareness of these dangers is beginning to cause severe political problems in several NATO countries.

Yet the obvious alternatives present their own dangers and difficulties. To return to the declared policy of massive retaliation, in the current state of the nuclear balance, would obviously lack all credibility; while to attempt to match Russian conventional strength by building up NATO's own conventional forces to an adequate level is as unrealistic, politically and economically, as it was at the time of the Lisbon Goals. A new conceptual approach to the defence of Western Europe is clearly essential; and in this context modern technology offers remarkable possibilities for the strengthening of conventional striking power without substantial numerical increases in forces and equipment.

An important aim of British defence policy must therefore be to maintain, and eventually to improve, the strength of its contribution to the conventional defence of Western Europe. In due course it should be possible to redeploy to Europe the military resources at present committed to non-NATO tasks in Northern Ireland, the South Atlantic and Hong Kong. At the same time developments in information technology and precision-guided munitions will make it possible to enhance the defensive capability of the British Army of the Rhine without the need for substantial increases in the number of troops deployed, which would certainly mean a return to some form of compulsory military service. Although this might be desirable on both social and military grounds, it is unlikely that a government of any complexion would regard it as politically feasible.

The second element of Britain's contribution to the Western alliance is its nuclear striking force consisting of four Polaris submarines, each capable of striking at targets in the Soviet Union with sixteen long-range missiles equipped with nuclear warheads in the megaton range. Of these four submarines, one is constantly on station and at a high degree of combat readiness. These vessels and their missiles are normally assigned to the Supreme Allied Commander Europe, and their targets are determined by him. In a national emergency, however, it would be possible for the British Government unilaterally to resume the sole responsibility both for allocating the targets and firing the missiles.

This force, sometimes described as the 'independent nuclear deterrent', therefore has two distinct politico-military functions. In the first place it contributes to the overall power of the allied nuclear arsenal, the principal function of which is to deter the Soviet Union from using its conventional forces to attack Western Europe by posing the implicit threat of an early resort by NATO to the use of nuclear weapons. Although it can be argued that the American nuclear capability is so enormous that the relatively small British contribution is numerically irrelevant, this is to ignore the important psychological importance to the alliance of having a nuclear retaliatory capability outside the direct control of the United States. Its second function is to deter the Soviet Union from contemplating a nuclear attack upon the United Kingdom by posing the threat of instant British retaliation against Russian cities and military installations.

These conventional and nuclear forces, if kept at adequate strength and at an appropriate state of combat readiness, combine to provide an effective deterrent against Soviet attack or nuclear blackmail. Those who now advocate the unilateral renunciation of the nuclear element in this deterrent must therefore submit themselves to the intellectual discipline of constructing an alternative system of national security. At this stage it is appropriate to consider the underlying motives and arguments of the unilateralist school.

o   o   o

It has to be said, at the risk of being accused of witch-hunting, that a considerable number of those who advocate unilateral disarmament do so because they wish to see this country defenceless against the designs of the Soviet Union. To categorise them as 'Communists' or 'Marxists' is not an especially illuminating exercise. They are, however, agents of Soviet influence, whether conscious or unconscious, as they ply their trade in many disguises – as teachers, professors, television producers, civil servants and Members of Parliament. They manipulate and exploit the machinery of democracy with the single aim of destroying it. By exploiting the Campaign for Nuclear Disarmament they have brought their influence to bear upon a broad constituency ranging, as Sir Michael Howard has put it, 'from saintly men of penetrating intelligence to mindless fanatics impervious to reasoned argument'.

There are, of course, many who advocate unilateral nuclear disarmament from a depth of sincere conviction. They believe in the provision of effective arrangements for defence but argue that the British nuclear striking force is at best irrelevant and at worst potentially damaging to national security. The arguments which they deploy usually fall into one or more of three broad categories: moral, political and economic.

The moral argument rests upon the proposition that nuclear weapons are so appallingly and indiscriminately destructive that to use them in war is immoral, because their evil effect would be disproportionate to any good that might theoretically be secured by their use. This belief has impeccable antecedents in the traditional Christian formulation of the doctrine of the just war – specifically in the concepts of proportionality and discrimination. It is, of course, possible to argue that a nuclear weapon is no more immoral than any other weapon used to kill people. It is certainly difficult for a reasonable man to draw any valid moral distinction between nuclear weapons on the one hand and, on the other, chemical or microbiological agents, the high explosive and incendiary bombs which were used to destroy Coventry, Dresden and Hamburg or even the artillery shells which helped to reduce the abbey at Monte Cassino to a heap of rubble.

It would be perverse to reject the proposition that nuclear weapons are different, not merely in scale but in kind, from any other weapons of war, if only because of the potential genetic effects of nuclear radiation; and that their use as weapons of mass destruction against civilian populations would be immoral. There remains, however, the question of whether the *threat* of their use as a deterrent is also immoral. The position of some Christians is that the conditional intent in this case is no different from the action – that a threat to carry out an immoral act is as immoral as the act itself. This point of view, which is considered again later in this paper in the context of unilateralism, seems to take insufficient account of another important element in the doctrine of the just war: that concerning the justice of the aim.

To use a simple everyday analogy, there would seem to be a valid moral distinction between the behaviour of a man who threatens violence in defence of his own person or property and that of the man who does so in the commission of robbery or rape. Similarly, in the doctrine of the just war, as Julian Lider has pointed out in his book *On the Nature of War**, the justification most widely accepted throughout history (and in all belief systems) has been defence against aggression. The strategy of the Western alliance involves the threat of nuclear retaliation to deter a potential enemy from attacking the West, either with his own nuclear weapons or with his demonstrably superior conventional forces. The Soviet doctrine envisages that nuclear weapons might be used in any military conflict, including one in which their use became necessary to overcome the enemy's defences. In this context the moral objection to the possession of nuclear weapons as a deterrent seems to be less persuasive.

The political or strategic arguments for unilateral disarmament by the United Kingdom rest upon the proposition that the possession of nuclear weapons is intrinsically provocative, and that if Britain were to abandon them it would cease to be a

*Saxon Ho. 1978.

target for nuclear attack. This ignores the inconvenient historical fact that on the only occasion that nuclear weapons have been used in war, they were used against a country which had no capacity to retaliate. In any case, in the British context it is an obscure argument, since the British strategic nuclear striking force is submarine-based. It is therefore invulnerable to a pre-emptive strike directed at the territory of the United Kingdom. The cosy assumption that unilateral disarmament would in itself provide us with a nuclear sanctuary has very little basis in reality.

The economic arguments are even less convincing. The standard references to the 'crippling cost of nuclear weapons', with the corollary, spoken or implicit, that they are taking bread out of the mouths of the poor, are not easy to reconcile with the fact that the cost of maintaining the Polaris force is £126 million a year – that is to say, one-fifth of one per cent of the gross national product; or, to put it another way, substantially less than the annual budget of the London Borough of Camden. Much of the public misapprehension about the cost of nuclear weapons springs from the published estimates of the capital cost of a new generation of nuclear missiles – the Trident system – with which the Government proposes to replace Polaris.

It is this issue which has been the catalyst for the latest phase in the public debate about Britain's defence policy. The Labour Party has incorporated into its proposals for the defence of the United Kingdom the principal elements of unilateralism – the 'decommissioning' of the present Polaris missile force; the cancellation of the Trident programme; and the removal of all American nuclear weapons and nuclear bases from British soil. The Liberal–SDP Alliance accepts the need for a British nuclear striking force, but believes that Trident is the wrong way to provide it. They propose to examine the possibility of other delivery systems. The Trident programme is therefore at the heart of the argument about a future defence policy for this country.

○   ○   ○

The debate is taking place against a background of significant changes both in the pattern of international relations and in the technology of war. The United States, Britain's major NATO ally, is beginning to re-examine its own strategic assumptions in a way which might well weaken its present commitment to policies based on the defence of the European–Atlantic areas. Threats to American national interests have emerged in Central America, where the expansion of Soviet influence and the consequent destabilisation of the region is beginning to pose a direct threat to the mainland United States. At the same time the geopolitical and economic centre of gravity is beginning to shift from the European–Atlantic area to the Pacific Basin. Faced with these changes in the strategic calculus, a new mood of 'global unilateralism' is emerging in the United States. It is composed of a recognition of the global nature of the threat to the free world, together with a sense of frustration brought about by the inevitable problems of alliance politics. As a result, the US Administration, and the American people, are becoming increasingly impatient with European allies who seem to expect the United States to bear the largest burden of the defence of the free world, but who are openly unsympathetic and unsupportive when the United States is faced with a crisis elsewhere in the world. Developments in military science and technology are, at the same time, beginning to undermine all the familiar certainties about military strategy, whether nuclear or conventional. The possibilities reflected in space-based anti-missile defence, precision-guided weapons, directed energy, kinetic energy weapons and lasers are rapidly transforming the strategic environment.

If in these circumstances it is incumbent on everyone who thinks seriously about strategy and defence policy to re-examine their assumptions, it is especially important in the area of nuclear deterrence. To make an intelligent assessment of the role which Britain should seek to play in future nuclear strategy it is necessary to answer two basic questions. The first is, does the United Kingdom still need a nuclear striking force of its own? If the answer is yes, what sort of weapon system does it need?

∘   ∘   ∘

No one attempting to answer the question of whether Britain needs a nuclear striking force can ignore the fact that it already has one. In sheer practical terms the process of 'giving it up' poses problems which have never been sufficiently addressed, such as the disposal of the weapons and warheads already in existence. It is true that these difficulties are not insuperable; they indicate, however, that nothing to do with nuclear strategy is ever entirely simple or straightforward.

And one of the most important arguments about giving up that force concerns the whole context of international negotiations, especially in the field of arms control. It would surely be irresponsible to renounce such a capability without obtaining some major concession in return. This would, of course, have to be a concession from the Soviet Union which had a substantial effect on the overall East–West balance, not some derisory arrangement whereby in exchange for the abandonment by Britain of all its sixty-four ballistic missiles, the Soviet Union agreed to reduce its own stockpile of ICBM launchers from 1398 to 1334 – a suggestion which had a brief moment of glory after the visit of a group of Labour politicians to Moscow.

In any case, the abandonment of nuclear weapons is not an option which can be considered in a political vacuum. The British nuclear striking force is not only an independent nuclear deterrent usable in the last resort to threaten a potential attacker in the absence of a nuclear guarantee from any other power; it is an integral part of the whole complex of alliance strategy.

At the most obvious level, as Denis Healey used to argue, it provides a second centre of decision making which presents the leaders of the Soviet Union with an added complication in their strategic calculations. To put the matter at its crudest, if Soviet military planners contemplated an action of some kind in Western Europe which they believed would not cause the United States to threaten the use of its own nuclear striking forces, they could not be sure, however remote the possibility might seem to academic strategists, that the British Government would not threaten the use of its own nuclear striking force either in isolation, or possibly in collaboration with the third centre of decision making, France.

This line of argument sometimes leads to what is known as the 'catalytic' theory of nuclear deterrence which, put in its simplest form, envisages that if a situation arose in which the European nuclear powers believed that vital national or regional interests were at stake, but in which the United States was reluctant to use the threat of its own nuclear weapons, the threat or the use of French or British nuclear weapons would have the catalytic effect of forcing the United States into the equation. This is not a contingency which is, in reality, likely to arise, but it indicates the extent to which British nuclear weapons are already tightly woven into the whole fabric of Western defence and deterrence.

Finally, there is the argument that the United States feels understandably reluctant to carry the whole burden of moral responsibility for deterring the Soviet Union from military attack by the threat of nuclear weapons and wishes to count on the support of at least one of its allies. The French, of course, are not members of the integrated military structure of NATO; Britain therefore provides the United States with its only close support in the nuclear confrontation.

To these considerations of the collective security of the Western alliance must be added the not inconsiderable possibility that Britain's nuclear striking force might pose an independent deterrent against an attack upon this country or its vital interests. It has been fashionable over the years to suggest that there are no circumstances in which the United Kingdom might credibly threaten to use its own nuclear weapons if the United States were not prepared to threaten the use of theirs. Although this may have been true at certain stages in the development of nuclear strategy, it is now an extremely dubious proposition.

In the first place, it is by no means out of the question that there might arise in the not too distant future a situation in which, either through the further development of space-based defence systems or through bilateral arms control agreements, there might be some kind of 'stand-off' between the Super-powers – namely, a situation in which the use of nuclear weapons by either of them against the other had become demonstrably ineffective and therefore without credibility as a threat. There were premonitions of this at the meeting between Mr Reagan and Mr Gorbachev at Reykjavik last year when there were on the table, if only for a short time, proposals that the United States and the Soviet Union should give up all ballistic nuclear missiles and withdraw from Europe all intermediate-range nuclear weapons. It is by no means out of the question that these proposals might be revived, and possibly adopted.

In these circumstances, there might be a temptation on the part of Soviet planners to calculate that they could use conventional forces to attain limited objectives in Western Europe – and even conceivably in the United Kingdom – without the danger of intervention by the United States. However dogmatically Western theorists might dismiss the possibility that a British government would threaten to use, much less actually use, nuclear weapons in these circum-stances, no responsible or sane Soviet planner would be likely to base his calculations on such an uncertain assumption.

Furthermore, it must now be accepted that the strategy of nuclear non-proliferation has, for all practical purposes, failed. For some time only five powers – the five permanent members of the United Nations Security Council, namely the United States, the Soviet Union, France, Britain and China – possessed nuclear weapons. In these circumstances, the only obvious and clear nuclear threat to the West has been posed by the Soviet Union. For various reasons which it is unnecessary to examine here in detail, the People's Republic of China has not posed and still does not pose a military threat to the West.

More recently, however, it has become clear that several

other countries now have the capacity to produce and stockpile nuclear weapons and to construct effective if limited delivery systems. Indeed, there is very strong evidence that a number of countries, such as India, Israel and South Africa, already have a nuclear weapons capability either laboratory-tested or, in the case of South Africa and India, possibly fully tested. Countries such as Pakistan, Japan and Argentina undoubtedly have the scientific and industrial base to construct a modest nuclear striking force if they should believe it in their national interest to do so. Furthermore, even if this were not sufficiently destabilising, there is strong evidence that Middle Eastern countries such as Iraq and Libya have been making strenuous attempts over a number of years to acquire nuclear weapons of their own. In these circum-stances, the abandonment by Britain of its own nuclear capability is no simple matter.

It must be considered not only in the context of the major East–West confrontation, but in the context of a world in which the spread of nuclear weapons becomes more and more likely as the technology of their manufacture becomes simpler and more widely known. There is, therefore, a strong presumption that unless there are more powerful arguments for the abandonment of the existing British nuclear weapons capacity than at present exist, and unless some clear advan-tage in the field of international relations and arms control negotiations could be obtained in exchange, Britain should certainly retain a capacity for nuclear deterrence.

There is, in any case, a more powerful and subtle argument against any proposal for unilateral nuclear disarmament. The two principal arguments deployed by those who wish to abandon Britain's nuclear capacity are the practical matter of cost and the more sophisticated case of the moral imperative. The cost argument can be fairly simply dealt with. In the first place, the running costs of our existing nuclear striking force are minimal. They represent only a very small percentage of our total defence budget and the saving from decommission-ing the current Polaris fleet, as already pointed out, would be marginal. The capital cost of replacing Polaris would, of course, be much more substantial. However, even taking the worst financial case, the possible cost of the replacement now envisaged – the Trident system – is not as ruinous as it has been represented to be, especially if it were amortised over the years of the development and deployment of the system.

The principal argument of the unilateralists about the effect of the savings if this system were cancelled does not really stand up to close examination. The more extreme argument of the 'peace people' is that this money should be devoted instead to good works, such as the relief of famine in the Third World and a redistribution of global resources. Anyone who has studied the matter with any degree of political objectivity knows that the transfer of resources which this implies is no simple matter; in any case it can be fairly clearly demonstrated that even if the entire sum saved from Trident were devoted to aid to the Third World, the impact on development problems would be insignificant.

The less extreme argument is that at present advanced by the leadership of the Labour Party – namely that the savings from the adoption of a non-nuclear defence policy would be devoted to improving our conventional defences. It can, however, be fairly clearly demonstrated that the increment to our land forces, air forces, surface or submarine fleets which would be made possible by cancellation of Trident would be no more than marginal and would certainly not enable us to pose, in the face of the current Russian threat, a conventional deterrent. The addition of an armoured division in Germany, or a few frigates or fighter aircraft to the Navy or the Air Force, is unlikely to provide for Russian planners the same problems as they have to contemplate when confronted with a modern and effective nuclear strike force.

Finally, it is necessary to examine the effect on the Atlantic alliance of a decision by Britain to abandon its nuclear capability. It is in this context that the moral argument has once again to be considered. If it is suggested that we should give up our nuclear striking force because the use of nuclear weapons is immoral, and because the threat of their use is equally immoral, this proposition requires closer examination. In the first place, even if the use of nuclear weapons is seen to be immoral – and this is a complicated argument in itself – it is by no means as clear that the threat of their use is equally immoral. Many distinguished churchmen argue that the use of force of any kind can be morally distinguished from the conditional intent to use it. This is, however, a profound moral and ethical argument about which even distinguished theologians differ.

Nevertheless, anyone who holds the view that we should abandon our own nuclear striking force because its use or the threat of its use is immoral, must surely regard it as equally immoral to rely on a nuclear guarantee from any other country. In that case, two consequences follow. The first is that we could not allow the United States to use any installation in this country as a base from which to deliver its own nuclear weapons. This is the conclusion which the Labour Party has now apparently drawn. Such a conclusion, however, carries with it a further and even more serious corollary. If it is accepted that we cannot rely upon the use or threat of the use of nuclear force because it is intrinsically immoral, then, quite clearly, it is entirely illogical to continue to be a member of NATO since its entire strategy is based upon the ultimate threat of nuclear retaliation. The logical consequence, therefore, of a decision to adopt a non-nuclear strategy is withdrawal from NATO and the adoption of a foreign policy of neutrality or non-alignment. To pretend otherwise is profoundly dishonest. The Labour Party leadership has not, so far, accepted this logic – arguing that, like Norway or Luxemburg, Britain can remain an effective member of NATO without nuclear weapons or nuclear bases. While this might satisfy a country aspiring to no greater influence in the world than that of Norway or Luxemburg, it is unlikely to appeal to those who believe that Britain should not be content to play a tame or minor role in the affairs of the free world.

Meanwhile a substantial element in the Labour Party is prepared to accept the logic of unilateralism and to disengage from the Western alliance. It is an element which would have an influential voice if the Labour Party under its present leadership ever succeeded in forming a government.

In any case, it is extremely unlikely that the United States would be prepared to contemplate a situation in which its major ally renounced its nuclear weapons and removed American bases from British territory while the American Government and people continued to bear the cost and moral responsibility of defending the very country which had implemented these policies. The inevitable result of a policy of unilateral nuclear disarmament by this country is, therefore, to weaken and eventually to unravel NATO and to accelerate the American tendency to withdraw into Fortress America, abandoning the entangling alliance which is already of dubious value to many Americans; and which, in the event of unilateral nuclear disarmament by Britain, would be seen as an almost unlimited liability.

If, therefore, it seems sensible to conclude that Britain needs a nuclear striking force, not only now but in the future, it is necessary to decide what kind of system it should be.

∘   ∘   ∘

Most observers agree that the present Polaris system, although effective for the moment, will not continue to be so for much longer. With four boats in commission we can only guarantee to have one on station at any given time and given the improvements in anti-submarine warfare which are likely to take place in the coming years it is doubtful that we should continue to rely for very much longer on a marginal capacity of that kind.

With one boat on station carrying sixteen missiles equipped with the improved Chevaline warheads, there is still sufficient potential penetrative and destructive power to cause doubts in the mind of any Soviet planner. However, faced with a constant improvement in anti-submarine warfare, a credible deterrent needs to have greater range – not necessarily to strike at more distant targets from present operational areas, but primarily to provide greater flexibility in the extent of the operational areas themselves. Furthermore the current Polaris system, even with the Chevaline warhead, is unlikely to be able to penetrate an enhancement of the present ABM system deployed around Moscow, much less the sophisticated, possibly space-based, strategic defence systems of the future.

So much has been said and written, much of it notably uninformed, about the US Strategic Defense Initiative (SDI), or 'Star Wars' as it has been called by the headline writers, that there has been a tendency to ignore the work which the Soviet Union is doing in this field. For many years the Soviet Union has been conducting advanced research in the field of lasers, directed energy weapons and kinetic energy weapons. Although the United States is undeniably well ahead in some aspects of space-based defence research and certainly has the potential to widen the gap between it and the Soviet Union, there is little doubt that in some areas the Soviet Union itself is well advanced. Furthermore the phased array radar system at Krasnoyarsk, in spite of persistent Soviet denials, is certainly more consistent with the kind of radar system that would be needed for an advanced space-based system than for any of the antiballistic missile systems permitted under the current ABM Treaty between the Soviet Union and the United States.

Some of the best scientific and technical minds in the Soviet Union are currently engaged in the research and development of strategic defence systems; and the intensive Soviet campaign against the Strategic Defense Initiative almost certainly arises from a fear that the scientific and economic resources of the United States would enable the Americans to overtake the Russian effort and to deploy effective strategic defence systems long before the Soviet Union could do so.

It would be prudent for all Western planners, including those who advise the British Government, to take account of the possibility that early in the next century the Soviet Union will be in a position to deploy advanced antiballistic missile systems including space-based defences. These will probably be capable not only of destroying land-based ballistic missiles from the boost phase through the mid-course to the re-entry phase, but also of destroying submarine-launched missiles in the mid-course and re-entry phases, and possibly even of destroying cruise missiles by using some of the techniques which will undoubtedly emerge from strategic defence research.

When, therefore, an earlier British government came to consider the replacement of Polaris it had all these factors to take into account – the range and penetrability of the existing missiles, the continued reliability and serviceability of the boats, and the inevitable improvement in Soviet techniques of anti-submarine warfare and defence against ballistic and air-breathing delivery systems. There is, in addition, a consideration which is too often ignored; it is the importance of having, wherever possible, a common nuclear weapons system with our major ally the United States. This has been at the heart of the development of all our deterrent systems from bombers through the abortive Skybolt system to Polaris, Poseidon, the Trident C4 and now the current plan for the Trident D5.

The Trident C4 was in fact quite well suited to the military requirements of the United Kingdom. The missile had a range of over 4000 miles, thus increasing the operational range of the submarines. Each missile could deliver up to eight warheads, in the form of multiple independently guided re-entry vehicles (MIRVs) each of which could be directed on to a separate target with an accuracy of about 500 yards. The extra range of the C4 made it unlikely to become vulnerable to foreseeable improvements in Soviet anti-submarine warfare, and the fact that each submarine could carry up to 128 warheads meant that even one boat on station would have the capacity to penetrate present and predictable Soviet defences.

The D5, of course, is a very different matter. Each missile will be armed with up to fourteen warheads with an accuracy even greater than that of the C4. It is, indeed, often argued that the D5 is a system of greater accuracy and sophistication than Britain really needs and that it constitutes a provocation to the Soviet Union. Yet, clearly, it would not have made very much sense for the United Kingdom to go ahead with its plans to acquire the C4 system after the United States had decided to move to the D5. Indeed it is unlikely that the C4 option would have remained available.

There are, in addition, other arguments in favour of the D5 system. One is its flexibility in the arms control process. As Admiral of the Fleet Lord Lewin, a former Chief of the Defence Staff, has pointed out, it would be possible in certain circumstances to put twelve missiles instead of sixteen in the submarine and leave four tubes empty. Similarly it would be possible to vary the warhead content in each missile. All these variations would be available in the context of any future arms control agreement and some would be clearly verifiable by the Soviet Union, using its own national means of surveillance.

The principal argument in favour of the Trident D5, however, is in the context of its effectiveness against future Soviet strategic defences, especially those around Moscow. In analysing Britain's requirement for a future nuclear strike force, it is important to remember that Britain does not need, even if it could achieve it, what is known as a first-strike capability. That is, it does not need a nuclear striking force capable of attacking and destroying the Soviet offensive capability. It needs only a second strike capability, that is, the ability to pose the threat of unacceptable devastation to the Soviet Union in the case of a Soviet attack. This means a counter-city capability rather than a counter-force capability – the requirement is to pose a threat to the Soviet population, centres of government and economic production of a kind which would make any Russian attack an unacceptable risk.

This postulates the sombre but inescapable need to be able to strike at the main centre of Soviet government, military command and national administration – in other words, Moscow. Now, the Soviet Union already has, under the terms of the existing ABM Treaty with the United States, a ballistic missile defence system deployed to protect its capital city. The Russians are constantly upgrading and enhancing this system, and it is already at a stage in development which would give it a considerable defensive capability against the current Polaris system. If the Soviet Union continues to improve its ballistic missile defences around Moscow, and furthermore, if it develops a strategic defence system depending partly upon space-based systems, it might be possible to achieve a defensive system which would be guaranteed to destroy up to 90 per cent of an incoming ballistic missile attack.

In the case of Polaris, even with a Chevaline warhead, this would be a significant attrition rate; but with the D5 Trident system, on the assumption that we shall still have four boats, the British nuclear striking force would be theoretically capable of delivering 896 MIRVs at selected Soviet targets. Therefore, even if the Soviet Union were capable of knocking out 90 per cent of this missile force, there would still be approximately 90 warheads guaranteed to reach a target. As Britain needs only to ensure a second-strike rather than a first-strike capability it would not be important which target was reached, as each would be a centre of command, population or economic production.

Even if there were only one boat on station, it would still be able to deliver 224 MIRVed missiles of which, even against the most effective of Soviet strategic defences, more than twenty missiles would still arrive at their targets. If, therefore, the United Kingdom is to have a strategic nuclear strike force which is capable of posing a credible second-strike threat to the Soviet Union it will be necessary, in the context of the probable anti-submarine warfare and strategic defence techniques of the early years of the next century, to have a system with capabilities very similar to those of the Trident D5.

A number of other alternatives for a Polaris replacement have been put forward from time to time, most notably by the Liberal–SDP Alliance. The possibility most frequently canvassed is a cruise missile which would be capable of being fired from a mobile platform such as a submarine. Although it is by no means certain that this would be very much cheaper than a Trident missile, it would, according to those who support the idea, release us from our dependence on the

United States in that the missile could be manufactured in the United Kingdom. It is also suggested that this would be less provocative to the Soviet Union while being equally capable of reaching its target.

While these arguments might be valid under the current state of Soviet defences, it is doubtful whether a cruise missile would pose a credible second-strike threat to the Soviet Union in the context of the kind of missile defence systems which will exist in the next century. In any case, the cruise missile, although it might for some time be invulnerable to the kind of techniques being developed for the destruction of ballistic missiles, is, by the very nature of an air-breathing delivery system, relatively slow and therefore vulnerable to less sophisticated defensive systems.

Various other proposals have been put forward, including the possibility of collaboration with the French – the main effect of which, according to those who propose it, would be to reduce the United Kingdom requirement to three boats, and possibly make available the French M4 missile in place of Trident, thereby reducing our reliance on the United States. All previous attempts at multinational nuclear collaboration have, however, demonstrated that the political problems are extremely difficult to overcome. Furthermore, much of Britain's current nuclear weapons capability relies upon technology acquired from the United States, of a kind which it would not be possible to share in the context of an Anglo-French agreement. In any case, it is not immediately evident how reliance on France would be preferable to reliance on the Americans.

The inescapable conclusion is that the present situation is too precarious and the future too uncertain to justify the abandonment of a strategic asset which still has a sound political and military justification. It is, of course, possible that there might emerge, in the course of the next fifteen years or so, international agreements in the field of arms control which would materially change the strategic context. Until this happens, however, it would clearly be irresponsible for any British government unilaterally to abandon its nuclear weapons capability. The weight of logic and evidence suggests that previous governments have made the correct decision in choosing the Trident D5 system as the successor to Polaris. It provides a basis of common procurement with the United States; it provides a credible nuclear striking force with sufficient range, throw weight and penetrative power to guarantee to threaten unacceptable damage on the centres of Soviet government even in the context of ballistic missile defence improvements; and it provides the extra operational flexibility which is likely to be necessary as anti-submarine warfare techniques improve over the next twenty years.

Furthermore, it reverses a disadvantageous trend in the development of our nuclear striking force. Each new system since the bomber – Polaris in its original mode and subsequently Chevaline – has actually reduced the number of targets at which we can strike. Trident D5 significantly increases that number.

o   o   o

It seems clear, in cold logic, that the policy of the present government of basing its defence policies upon the foundation of effective nuclear deterrence is sound and prudent. In matters concerning nuclear weapons, however, logic is often driven out by emotion – especially by that most powerful of all emotions, fear. It is fear of the nuclear holocaust, rather than a more general revulsion against war, which has fuelled the current intensive phase in the pressure for arms control and disarmament. This pressure springs from real and genuine concerns, a fact which must be recognised by any democratically elected government. Effective defence policies must therefore go hand in hand with the pursuit of balanced, multilateral and verifiable arms control agreements. In this context it is important to recognise that it is *war* which we seek to avoid, not just nuclear war.

One of the fallacies at the heart of the almost universal fear of nuclear weapons is the belief, carefully fostered by the peace movements, that we are on the brink of an apocalyptic disaster, which will lay waste to the world, annihilate its inhabitants in millions and bequeath to future generations a legacy of mental and physical disease. That is certainly what would happen if there were a major nuclear war; but there is probably less danger of a war involving the great powers now than there was on many occasions before the nuclear weapon was invented. The evidence of history is that arms races alone do not cause wars. The causes of war are subtle and intricate; they derive from political, economic and even psychological forces which eventually lead a power or group of powers to calculate that by using its military strength it can achieve gains which will outweigh the costs of war.

So far as the major armed confrontation in the world today is concerned – that between the Soviet Union and its allies on the one hand and the Western alliance on the other – the advent of nuclear weapons has profoundly and irrevocably altered the calculus. There is no political prize which either side could conceivably regard as being worth the risk of a nuclear war. Now that the great powers have the capacity to inflict intolerable damage and suffering upon each other, *and as long as each side knows that the other possesses that power*, the possibility of war between them is, in fact, remote.

This is not to suggest that this situation is either desirable or permanently acceptable. Madmen have risen to positions of absolute power before, and they may do so again; the significance of the current uneasy confrontation is that, if the Superpowers were plunged into a war, the consequences for the rest of the world would be almost unimaginably dreadful – partly because they have amassed a stockpile of weapons with such potential for destruction that few people, any-where, would escape the effects entirely. The problem which we face, therefore, is how to reduce those stockpiles to a level at which the capacity to deter a potential enemy from going to war remains, without posing the threat of global disaster if the deterrent should ever fail.

In the past, the function of nuclear weapons has been as a mutually cancelling deterrent, maintained solely to insure each side against attack by the other. This situation was

known variously as the balance of terror, the nuclear stalemate or, by strategic analysts, as 'mutual assured destruction'
(usually abbreviated, much to the delight of the antinuclear
lobby, to the acronym MAD).

With the emergence of new weapons of great accuracy and
penetrative power, strategic theorists have begun to discuss
the possibility of disarming strikes in which nuclear missiles
would be used not to threaten the indiscriminate destruction
of the enemy's cities, but to destroy his capacity to retaliate.
Thus it is sometimes suggested that a nuclear war might now
be 'winnable'. Variations on this bizarre theme include
speculation about the possibility of a limited nuclear war, in
which an exchange of nuclear weapons between adversaries
might be restricted as to their number, type or the geographical
area in which they were used. One of the results of this
strange excursion into fantasy has been to exacerbate the
natural fear of nuclear war and to provide a powerful impetus
to anti-war and antinuclear protest movements in the West.

Meanwhile, however, the built-in momentum of nuclear
weapons development continues. Since late 1981, the Soviet
Union has begun test flights of two new land-based intercontinental ballistic missiles, a new generation of strategic
manned bombers and a new series of cruise missiles.
President Reagan has authorised the deployment of a new
intercontinental system, MX, and the United States has, with
the consent of its allies, deployed cruise missiles and a new
generation of intermediate-range ballistic missiles in Western
Europe.

This constant accretion of nuclear weapons by the existing
nuclear powers – sometimes referred to as 'vertical proliferation' – is now in danger of being matched by the development
of 'horizontal proliferation' – the spread of nuclear weapons
outside the five major powers which now possess them.

In an attempt to eliminate the obvious dangers of horizontal
proliferation, a treaty was concluded in 1967 and subsequently signed by and ratified by more than a hundred states.
Under the terms of the Nuclear Non-Proliferation Treaty,
nuclear weapon states agree not to transfer, and non-nuclear

weapon states not to receive, nuclear weapons or the technology for their manufacture. The Non-Proliferation Treaty is only one example of the numerous attempts which have been made to control the power of the nuclear weapon since it made its first appearances at Hiroshima and Nagasaki. As early as 1946 the US Government put forward the Baruch Plan for the establishment of an international authority to control all atomic fuel and facilities and to supervise the destruction of all nuclear weapons. The Soviet Union rejected the Baruch Plan and put forward one of its own which was rejected by the United States on the grounds that it made inadequate provision for international inspection – an issue, incidentally, which has bedevilled arms control negotiations ever since. In 1959 the Antarctic Treaty prohibited all military and nuclear activities in the area; in 1963 the Partial Nuclear Test Ban Treaty banned the testing of nuclear weapons in space, in the atmosphere and underwater (but not underground); in 1967 a treaty was signed prohibiting the stationing of missiles in outer space; and in 1971 the positioning of nuclear devices on the sea-bed was forbidden.

In 1971 the first of the Strategic Arms Limitation agreements (SALT I) sought, without great success, to place limits on both the offensive and defensive nuclear missile systems of the United States and the Soviet Union. In 1974 the two Superpowers agreed to the cessation of underground nuclear tests above a yield of 150 kilotons (the equivalent of 150,000 tons of high explosive); and in 1979 a second Strategic Arms Limitation Treaty (SALT II) made another attempt to limit American and Russian delivery systems. It has, however, never been ratified, it has been repeatedly contravened by the Soviet Union, and it has not been, for all practical purposes, renounced by the United States.

Whatever might be the value of these various agreements (and it is certainly greater than radical disarmament movements suggest), they suffer from two major weaknesses. The first is that they have never been universal in their application. Two of the five nuclear powers (France and China) have taken no part in the negotiations and are not formally bound by the treaties. The second weakness is that no provision has been made for actual disarmament – for the reduction of existing levels of nuclear weapons. This has now become a matter of great urgency.

Although the 'numbers game' – the attempt to judge the nuclear balance on a numerical basis – is academic, and, in the context of the massive destructive power on both sides, largely irrelevant, a continuing competition in nuclear weapons contains a number of inherent dangers. In the first place it distorts national economies by diverting valuable technological and human resources; secondly it perpetuates a situation in which mechanical accident or gross political misjudgement could have catastrophic consequences; and, most important of all, an upward spiral of nuclear weapons development poses the threat that, at some stage, one side or the other may perceive that it has superiority, or that the other side might be about to achieve it – the 'window of vulnerability' theory. At such a stage the danger of a surprise or pre-emptive attack is substantially increased.

A new and equally destabilising factor has been introduced into the equation by the recent growth in the West of radical protest movements demanding one-sided disarmament and the dismantling of the Western alliance. The inescapable consequence of what they are demanding would be to make nuclear war more, rather than less likely. An uncontrolled, unbalanced, downward spiral of disarmament would create the same dangerous instabilities as an uncontrolled upward spiral. Furthermore, unilateral disarmament by the West would clearly remove any modest incentive which at present exists for the Soviet Union to engage in binding international agreements.

There are signs that the great powers are at last beginning to approach the problem of resolving the nuclear dilemma with a properly serious sense of purpose. Since 1981, the Soviet Union and the United States have been discussing the problem of intermediate-range nuclear forces (INF), in an attempt to reduce the number of missiles designed for theatre use – that is to say, designed to destroy military installations and other targets in Europe. The major threat to the West in this context is the Russian SS20, a powerful, accurate and mobile missile system of which 270 are now aimed at Western Europe. In an attempt to counter this threat NATO has deployed American cruise missiles, as well as a new version of the Pershing ballistic missile, in certain countries of the alliance.

In the INF talks the United States has proposed the so-called 'zero option', under which the NATO deployments would be abandoned in exchange for a Russian undertaking to destroy all its SS20s. In the meantime the Soviet Union has achieved a substantial superiority in short-range nuclear systems in Europe. The old Strategic Arms Limitation Talks have, significantly, been renamed START (Strategic Arms Reduction Talks); and when the talks opened in Geneva in June 1982, the United States immediately proposed reductions of nuclear warheads by one-third and of ballistic missiles by a half, with further reductions to follow. So far the Soviet Union has been unable to agree. More far-reaching proposals were discussed at Reykjavik last year, but they were aborted by the insistence of the Soviet Union that the United States should abandon its research into space-based ballistic missile defence systems (SDI) and the refusal of the Americans to do so.

The process of bringing the nuclear weapon under control is likely to be a long and difficult one, requiring the constant exercise of political wisdom and intellectual subtlety. The facile slogan 'Ban the Bomb' serves only to exacerbate irrational fears and stimulate unrealistic hopes. The knowledge of how to construct, test and use nuclear weapons exists; and there can never again be a certainty that, even if all existing nuclear weapons were destroyed, someone in the future, faced with the prospect of defeat in a conventional war, would not reconstruct and use a nuclear weapon. Furthermore, even if it were possible for all nations to engage in some collective act of self-induced amnesia, and banish nuclear technology from the human consciousness, the world would not necessarily be a safer place. We would all then be at the mercy of any aggressor with powerful conventional armed forces, undeterred by the prospect of nuclear devastation. Those who declaim passionately about the horrors of nuclear war tend to forget that conventional war too is cruel, destructive and barbaric. This may not be entirely unconnected with the fact that the great majority of those who are most vociferous in their demands for nuclear disarmament have never experienced a conventional war.

o   o   o

The nuclear dilemma contains an inherent paradox. The nuclear weapon has injected a new dimension into the concept of war as a means of settling international disputes. It is generally agreed that a nuclear war would bring with it such appalling devastation that no nation state could conceivably hope to achieve any proportionate political aim by embarking on it. So long as nuclear weapons exist, furthermore, political leaders are less likely to engage in wars of any kind for fear that they might escalate into the nuclear dimension. The task is to devise a system of deterrence at substantially lower levels, so that, in the dreadful event that deterrence should fail, the result would not be universal annihilation. This state of affairs is more likely to be achieved by careful and patient negotiation than by quixotic acts of unilateral disarmament. The background of the nuclear dilemma underlines the sombre truth that in the complicated world of international relations, where the choices are made which may, in the end, mean the difference between war and peace, there are no 'quick fixes' or easy solutions. This does not, however, absolve international statesmen from the need to search for long-term alternatives to the present dangerous confrontation.

Nor does it absolve the elected government of this country from the duty to provide an effective defence policy while the search continues. Thomas Hobbes and his Sovereign Power may not strike a sympathetic chord in the hearts and minds of modern political activists; but there is another, more contemporary, way of delivering his message: 'Once we cut expenditure to the extent where our security is imperilled, we have no houses, we have no hospitals, we have no schools. We have a heap of cinders.' That was the view expressed in the House of Commons in March 1969 by Denis Healey, then the Labour Government's Defence Secretary, and now its principal spokesman on foreign affairs.

A Personal Viewpoint on a Dangerous World

Bruce Kent

1 Introduction: A Religious Perspective

> 'The War Horse is a vain hope for victory:
> by its great strength it cannot save.'
>
> Psalm 33

If this is to be a personal viewpoint, then it has to start from a religious basis. Others with different perspectives can and do come to the same conclusions. I can only describe what I see.

I see a world obsessed with military security. It is an obsession with one aspect of security only, that of exterior military invasion, and it is an obsession which now actually maximises insecurity as military technology creates ever more illusions.

Our obsession with military security is founded on three suppositions. The first is that the Soviet Union is an evil expansionist power with whom we can never have the 'normal' relations we now enjoy with West Germany, Japan and China. The second is that nuclear weapons fulfil some useful military function and that they actually protect us from this evil power. The third is that any restructuring of the present bloc positions in the world will only break down today's stalemate and risk new perils.

These delusions ensure that we run the world out of joint with the plans of our Creator. We make ourselves freeholders rather than trustees. Our judgements on others, especially the 'enemy', are ferocious, and on ourselves benign. We ridicule international agencies and assume that violence is the sensible way of coping with inter-state conflict. Far from acting as reconcilers, we pass on enemy stereotypes from generation to generation. The taking of hostages is not a new idea, but we have massively increased its scale and called it nuclear deterrence. It is supposed to have brought peace. Figs do not grow on thorn bushes. Peace cannot come from terror and threats of mass murder.

It is time that the delusions of the 'realists' were exposed once and for all and that idealism was finally accepted as the only genuinely realistic approach to peace. That there is another way of living is not just the distant dream of the prophet Micah: 'Nations shall not lift up sword against nation, neither shall they learn war any more.' We have to widen the circle of the possible. Those who pray 'Our Father' must believe that our humanity is more important than our differences. Those who pray 'Thy Kingdom come' have to believe in laying the foundations of that Kingdom here and now. One of the major obstacles on the road to the Kingdom is the militarisation of our world. The War Horse is no way to victory, let alone peace.

2 The Soviet Threat

The problem is very clear. We are dealing with a monolithic Soviet power. That's the real enemy. That's where the real threat is.
Michael Heseltine (Newbury 1983)

In these few words Michael Heseltine did indeed make very clear where the real risk is. It is in his mind and in the minds of thousands like him, in positions of power in Britain. It lies in the conviction that, monolithic, inexorable, ruthless, the Soviet Union is forever the enemy that waits to attack us. This is the first delusion of the 'realists'. Against this threat we are supposed to endlessly arm and re-arm. Those who have different perceptions must be either dupes or traitors. Since by definition they have to be the enemies of democracy there is no need to meet, in any rational way, objections which they may raise. This is the world of one dimension. There is no room for any other. Whether Mr Heseltine and his like actually believe in the views they express about the Soviet Union I do not know. The trade and cultural interests which now connect the two countries make it not unreasonable to doubt it. What I do believe is that there is nothing more useful, if you want to unite a people behind a government and a policy, than to convince them of perils awaiting from threats within and without. Hitler was an expert in this art.

From the earliest days of the revolution the Soviet Union has been seen as the threat by those in power in the West because it challenged fundamental positions about property and social control. Despite the brief period of World War II partnership, which ended with the dropping of the atomic bombs, the public have consistently been presented with a hostile image of the Soviet Union. Many actions that the Soviet Union itself has taken have made that presentation fairly easy. Defence is usually discussed only in terms of spending on weapons; rarely is consideration given to the reality of the threat or to the perceptions that 'the enemy' might have of our world.

Part of the problem lies in the difference between capabilities and intentions. I well remember a very reasonable Conservative minister, Francis Pym, telling a group of visitors that we should judge the Soviet Union by its capabilities and not by its intentions, because in the Soviet Union there was no possibility of open expression of public opinion. However, the Soviets, in his opinion, should judge the West by our intentions rather than our capabilities, because ours is a democratic society. Those double standards will no longer do.

It is clear enough that both the Soviet bloc and the American bloc, the two halves of our world, are perfectly capable of destroying our civilisation if they choose to do so. The destructive nuclear power at their disposal is effectively unlimited, and both blocs deploy vast conventional forces. Some claim to be able to assess intentions by examining the disposition of those forces. This does not always work very well. The American bases dotted around the world can either be seen as a security belt designed to prevent remorseless Soviet expansionism or they can be seen as the launching pads for an imperialist war on decent Soviet Socialism. It all depends on one's particular paranoia.

In terms of strategic nuclear deterrence, both blocs are grossly over-armed. Both have pursued ridiculous notions about the need for nuclear parity, although there is evidence now, especially on the Soviet side, that parity is no longer seen to be an objective that has to be unquestioned. Both retain such horrendous second-strike retaliatory capabilities, and will do so for the foreseeable future, that first-strike scenarios are still unreal. They will not remain so for ever as anti-submarine warfare techniques improve. Neither bloc has yet come to terms with the lesson of Chernobyl: every nuclear power station is a military hostage and the ability to hit one effectively turns non-nuclear states into nuclear ones.

There is no superpower short-cut which will enable the world to see an end to weapons of mass destruction overnight. It is politically quite unrealistic to expect one of the Superpowers to give up nuclear weapons entirely while the other still retains them. But there is a wide range of practical steps which could be taken here and now – none more important than a halt to any further nuclear tests. While we work towards a reduction of weapons we have also to think about the political tensions which produce them. The ultimate aim has to be a world free of the weapons of mass destruction. That world will have to have rather different ideas about the significance of national sovereignty.

It is today in the world of conventional weapons that there is room for more uncertainty and probably more propaganda. The picture has been regularly drawn of a NATO ever vulnerable to overwhelming Soviet conventional forces, particularly on the European front, and this has been used as one of the main justifications for having nuclear weapons. But how vulnerable are we really to a conventional attack? The NATO countries have twice the population of their Warsaw Pact counterparts and many times the economic strength. Moreover, although the political differences within NATO grow greater all the time, those tensions are small by comparison with the tensions between the Warsaw Treaty countries. I often wonder how those of the 'overwhelming conventional superiority' school of thought imagine Poland might react were an East–West wholly conventional conflict ever to break out. It seems unlikely that the Soviets could rely either on their Polish military allies or on the safety of their supply lines. In short, any assessment of strength has to take into account people and geography as well as weapons.

Do the Soviets have an overwhelming conventional superiority? Our Minister of Defence, George Younger, thinks so. On 9 November 1986, during the television programme 'Weekend World', he claimed that we now face 'a huge overwhelming preponderance of conventional weapons . . .' His timing was rather odd. On 6 November the International Institute for Strategic Studies had published its annual *Military Balance* which concluded that 'the conventional military balance is still such as to make military aggression a highly risky undertaking for either side.' This is not a new view. The Union of Concerned Scientists reported in February 1983 that 'NATO's forces are of sufficient size and quality to make an attack an expensive, risky and hence unattractive option for the Warsaw Pact.'

That the other view is so determinedly promoted is no surprise. No wonder it got major attention in the Western media after Reykjavik. The best way to throw a spanner in the works of a nuclear deal between the Superpowers is clearly to stress the perils of conventional military defeat awaiting us in a non-nuclear world.

What makes it so difficult to deal with all this seriously is the unwillingness of the realists of the Younger–Heseltine persuasion to produce a political scenario in which a conventional attack would make sense. The problems of administering the various countries of Western Europe after a conventional war which, even if victorious, would have destroyed the best part of the East as well as the West, are not discussed. Why the Soviets should wish to add such a vast problem to their already overcrowded political agenda is not easy to see. Nor is it clear what political accommodation would have to be reached with the Republic of China and its two million strong army to keep it quiet while Western Europe was being blown apart.

It is therefore quite clear that intentions and perceptions are just as important as physical capabilities. If head and weapon counts were all that mattered, the Americans would not have been defeated in Vietnam, and the Soviets would not now be bogged down in an unwinnable war in Afghanistan.

In fact the remorselessly expansionist view of post-1945 Soviet behaviour does not fit easily with the historical facts. The Soviet Union's decision not to intervene on behalf of its natural allies during the civil war in Greece was hardly expansionist behaviour. Nor was its departure from Austria. If the invasion of Afghanistan was really an expansionist threat to Western oil, then a straight line through Iran would have made much more sense than a detour via Kabul.

That the Soviet Union has global interests is perfectly obvious. But the list of its overseas failures is much longer than that of its successes. Most notably, it has failed to maintain its brotherly relationship with China. It has lost influence in a number of places including Yugoslavia, Indonesia, Egypt, Algeria, Ghana, Iraq and Sudan. Only six Third World countries are its devoted allies. Amongst its six allies in the Warsaw Treaty organisation there are clearly considerable differences. Romania shows a greater independence from its Soviet superpower partner than any NATO country from the United States. It has reduced its military budget, and has actually entered into an industrial agreement with the EEC. Two of the Warsaw Pact six were actually pro-Nazi during the last war, and Poland has an anti-Russian tradition going back, with good reason, for centuries. The GNP of the Soviet Union is perhaps 40 per cent that of the USA, which makes military expenditure comparisons based on

GNP dishonest. In numerical terms its direct military allies have populations totalling about 113 million, less than half of those of the NATO countries of Western Europe. Far from encouraging the countries where it does have influence into greater confrontation, the Soviet Union has actually urged moderation. It certainly did not win friends in some parts of the Arab world when it commended the recognition of the State of Israel's right to exist.

Much of the Soviet Union's behaviour in Europe is explained by its fear of a reunited, rearmed, and eventually nuclear Germany. Only two weeks after NATO admitted West Germany in 1955 the foundations of the Warsaw Treaty were laid; this was six years after the formation of NATO. Those who support the expansionist theory of Soviet behaviour often point to its delayed demobilisation in the post-war years. A recent study suggests that Khrushchev was telling the truth in 1960 when he claimed that by 1948 Soviet forces had been reduced from 11.4 to 2.9 million. It now seems hard to take seriously the view that at that time a Soviet invasion of Western Europe was contemplated. Invasion plans do not fit in well with the removal, as reparations from East Germany, of one track from most double-track railways. It seems rather more likely that a country which had been devastated to the gates of Moscow and which had just lost twenty million of its people might have had, in the years after 1945, other things on its mind.

One such preoccupation was the urge to build an atomic bomb. That Britain provided the United States with B29 atomic bomber bases in East Anglia, before the Soviet Union had produced its own bomb, must have stimulated that process. The Soviet Union's major political priority, then as now, was to build and maintain at all costs a buffer zone around its own territory by creating a series of client states which would be obliged to remain loyal, if necessary by force of arms. The buffer theory, the result of fear of outside threat, makes much more sense than any other. It also goes some way to explain the brutal treatment meted out to independent thinkers. Twice, in the first half of this century, the Soviet

Union has been invaded by hostile Western forces determined to destroy it, and Soviet policy post-1945 was clearly directed towards reducing the risk of a third attempt. Even General Rogers of NATO agreed in a speech in June 1986 that the threat faced by the West was not overt Soviet aggression, but Soviet intimidation.

How the Soviet Union has come to be seen as the evil enemy at the door is a matter for educationalists and psychologists as well as politicians. In part it was no accident. Anti-Sovietism has played a profound part in British thinking for many years. The bogus Zinoviev Letter* of 1924, promoted by our Foreign Office, ensured defeat for the Labour Party in the general election of that year. One of the weaknesses of Labour's defence position in 1987, over sixty years later, is that it still does not face up to the issue of the 'enemy'. This is the key issue. The Soviet Union has done many brutal things on its way from the world of the Tsars to the world of the Sputnik. We have ourselves hardly been innocents abroad over the course of the years. It is high time that we listened to the voice of George Kennan, highly respected US ex-Ambassador to the Soviet Union: 'The image of a Stalinist Russia, poised and yearning to attack the West . . . was largely the creation of the Western imagination . . .'

Thank God that a Gorbachev, who can both communicate and talk sense, has now appeared on the world scene. He must have shocked the Communist Party one-track old-timers in 1986 in Moscow when he told them that we are 'groping in the dark' towards an 'interdependent and in many ways integral world . . .'

But even if General Rogers and George Kennan are wrong to take an optimistic view of the Soviet stance, and there is a real threat of overt Soviet aggression, I will argue in Part Three that a defence policy which, if it ever goes wrong, will result in

---

*A letter allegedly written by Soviet politician Zinoviev, in which the British Communist Party was urged to revolt, contributed to the defeat of the Labour Government in 1924.

blowing up the best part of the world is hardly a sensible response.

The second great delusion of the 'realists' is that nuclear weapons are safe. I will show that, far from protecting us from the alleged Soviet threat, they actually endanger our security.

3 The Risks: Accidents and Mistakes

Accidental nuclear war is not a possibility because arrangements between the nuclear weapon states for its prevention are now very effective.
Foreign and Commonwealth Office

In any discussion about nuclear deterrence and the nuclear arms race a major difficulty arises about perceptions of risk. There are those, like the authors of the 'Short Guide to British Government Policy' from which the above quotation is taken, who believe that a war involving the use of nuclear weapons cannot happen because technical arrangements make that impossible.

There are many others who believe the opposite, and I am one of them. This different perception has a great deal to do with different ideas about security and threat. If you believe that you are crossing the road on a high wire rather than on the pavement you will have a different understanding of risks.

If a nuclear war by accident is not a possibility then it is not clear, since there is no point in deliberately starting one, why there should be any urgent need to reduce nuclear stockpiles. For instance, President Reagan correctly stated in February 1986: 'We want agreements that truly diminish the nuclear danger.' I am sure he is quite sincere. But what is the danger if deterrence is a secure system?

The fact is that no system which relies on complicated

mechanical and electrical systems as well as human beings can be fail-safe. I do not doubt that Soviet nuclear authorities convinced themselves and their citizens that nothing could go wrong with Chernobyl. It did, disastrously. We now know that at the time of the Challenger launch there were a few with doubts, but most of those involved – which includes all the public – were convinced that nothing could go wrong. It did, disastrously.

Some risks have to be taken. Others are unacceptable, and the greatest of those is that we might by miscalculation or accident start an uncontrollable nuclear war with catastrophic consequences for this and endless generations yet unborn. Professor Freedman of King's College, London, said in 1981 of the nuclear competition: 'to believe that this can go on indefinitely without major disaster requires an optimism unjustified by any historical or political perspective.' His is not the only sane voice. In 1983 the United Nations Institute for Disarmament Research reported that 'the system of deterrence is generally drifting towards becoming unstable.' There are even a number of senior Americans now who stress these risks in support of the Star Wars programme. Fred Iklé, Under-Secretary of Defense for the United States, told the Senate Armed Services Committee in 1985 that strategic defence systems (Star Wars) provide security 'by offering protection against accidental or irrational attack'. The kind of deterrence we have had up to now 'increases the risk of accidents or irrational acts'.

Either Iklé is right or our Foreign Office is right. They can't both be. It is worth remembering that supporters of Star Wars only claim it offers protection against ballistic missiles, and admit it does nothing whatever to guard against cruise missiles or free-falling nuclear bombs.

No one can be certain that disastrous miscalculations will never take place, especially as nuclear weapons and other weapons of mass destruction proliferate through the non-nuclear world. We actually have a Multilateral Treaty, the 1968 Treaty on the Non-Proliferation of Nuclear Weapons. It has not been signed by a number of potential nuclear weapon states and it is something of a poacher's charter in terms of the privileges which it gives to the nuclear states. It does oblige those states to negotiate in good faith an end to the nuclear arms race. But in fact all the nuclear powers have substantially augmented their arsenals since it was signed, which is hardly an example to the non-nuclear states. We now know that Israel (not a signatory) has its own nuclear weapons, and the Pakistan–Indian competition looks more threatening now that France is to resume talks with Pakistan about the supply of nuclear reprocessing facilities which would supplement the bomb material produced by its 1984 enrichment plant.

No one can forecast the spread of the proliferation process or the sequence of countries likely to be involved. But just as certainly no country will be able to deny the right to nuclear weapons to other states while claiming that they are essential for its own defence. Thus the hazards of war by miscalculation will progressively increase. The line between conventional and nuclear weapons gets dangerously narrowed as low-yield, high-accuracy nuclear weapons are produced. Last year saw two major student uprisings – in France and China. Suppose such an uprising took place in East Germany and was matched in West Germany and Poland, and civil disobedience took place on a major scale? No one can say that East–West armies might not find themselves as a consequence in a potentially nuclear conflict. Suppose that F1 11s striking Tripoli had destroyed the Soviet Embassy in Libya by error? The list of suppositions is as long as one's imagination cares to make them. The hard fact is that none can be ruled out as an impossibility, and one possibility is enough.

So it is with straightforward accidents. There has not been, in the forty years of nuclear weaponry, an accident which has resulted in nuclear explosion. There have though been very close calls. In 1961 a B52 bomber dropped a 24 megaton bomb on North Carolina and five of the six interlocking safety devices were set off by the fall. A major accident took place in 1956 at RAF Lakenheath which was not acknowledged until 1981. Commenting on the fact that there had not been a major nuclear release, an officer present at the time said: 'It was a combination of tremendous heroism, good fortune and the will of God.' In 1980 a fuel explosion resulted in a nine-megaton Titan warhead being hurled 600 feet into the air. In 1985 a Pershing II missile in West Germany actually caught fire within 250 yards of a store of nuclear warheads. More recently still a Soviet submarine with all its warheads on board sank, apparently after a fire or other damage to a missile tube, within a few hundred miles of the American East Coast. For those who want more information about past accidents and the risks of future ones, the Department of Politics of the University of Lancaster has produced a useful little pamphlet entitled 'It couldn't happen – could it?'

People do crack up, drink, take drugs and behave irrationally. Machines do break down. Computers do fail. Political situations do alter rapidly and unpredictably. However many safeguards there may be in a world of 50,000 nuclear weapons with a destructive power 6000 times that of World War II, one accident is too many. The comfort offered by our Foreign Office does not comfort me.

However, the 'realists'' refusal to acknowledge the risk of an accident involving a nuclear weapon is not the most serious charge against them. Even more dangerous is their belief that the use of a nuclear weapon could ever be a rational military option.

4   The Impossibility of Winning a Nuclear War

Operational conditions are only one part of the difficulty of limiting a nuclear war . . . the underlying dynamic would almost inevitably propel the conflict into larger and larger proportions.
Palme Report: Common Security (1982)

Some years ago Oliver Postgate did his best to redirect the English language. He wanted to stop people using the term 'weapon' in connection with nuclear bombs, rockets and the like and to substitute the word 'Geddon'. Geddon was derived from Armageddon – the time of total destruction. Weapons, he argued, were horrible instruments, but things that could be used to some rational purpose like trying to win a war. Geddons, on the other hand, could have no such purpose since, if ever used, they would mean defeat for all.

Postgate was right in his analysis, though the English language does not readjust so easily. Much of the present upset about the Labour Party's antinuclear policy derives from the outrage of those brought up on ideas of flexible response who still think that nuclear weapons serve some military purpose. They don't. Risking national and international suicide and mass murder is not a rational military purpose. Lord Kennet, for instance, writing in the *Guardian* on 19 December 1986 about Europe, declared that 'nuclear weapons are held by armies to prevent the adversary massing.' What can this mean? I doubt very much, with all the variety of conventional weapons which exist today, if 'massing' cannot be prevented by non-nuclear weapons. But how does Lord Kennet think that nuclear weapons can prevent massing unless there is a genuine willingness to use them? If they were ever to be used he cannot believe that the result would not be a high risk of an insane general nuclear exchange. Lord Kennet is not alone. A barrage of expert commentators have recently said or implied the same sort of thing. The SDP shift from 'No first use' to 'No early use' is simply a clever piece of confusion. The trouble is that, brought up on flexible response and first-use nuclear strategies, our experts cannot really get them out of their minds. Labour, much more on the right lines than either the Conservatives or the Alliance, actually feeds this illusion by stressing that money for defence not spent on nuclear weapons will instead be spent on conventional weapons. But these are not alternative systems of defence. The nuclear 'weapon' is a gun that fires both ways.

The language of deterrence, as fed to the general population, has been used in ways designed to confuse. Deterrence used to mean having nuclear weapons so that no one would ever use a nuclear weapon. It is an interesting idea that has given employment to a generation of moral theologians, and the logic was that every country ought to get its nuclear weapons as soon as possible. Such weapons were not meant for use but for threat. A devastating retaliatory strike would greet any country using nuclear weapons.

The Ministry of Defence used to assure us that if Polaris is ever used it will have failed. That language does not now apply to a whole range of tactical nuclear weapons. Our own Ministry of Defence says of cruise missiles that 'the aim of using [them] would be to persuade the Russian leadership, even at the eleventh hour, to draw back.' They have an operational function in the view of the MOD, and that must mean that the MOD believes that a limited nuclear war remains a possibility. NATO certainly does. Lord Carrington, no hawk in any respect, said that NATO relies on nuclear weapons 'to provide credible retaliatory capabilities if deterrence fails and we are attacked . . .'

He has to say that sort of thing until the policy changes. This is not to suggest that he wants a war. But he does believe that nuclear weapons have an operational purpose. Lord Mountbatten most certainly did not. In 1979 he said that he had never found credible the idea that nuclear weapons could be used in field warfare 'without triggering an all-out nuclear exchange leading to the final holocaust.' George Kennan, the American ex-Ambassador, said in 1981: 'to my mind the nuclear bomb is the most useless weapon ever invented. It can be employed to no rational purpose.'

But these voices are not yet taken seriously. As part of the major intervention into British politics by the representatives of the present, somewhat disgraced, American administration, Richard Perle, Assistant Secretary of Defense, declared on Radio 4 recently that he would use whatever weapons were necessary, including nuclear, in order 'to prevail'. In 1982, Casper Weinberger, Secretary of Defense, said that he did not believe a nuclear war to be winnable, but should deterrence fail, 'we are not planning to lose'. In 1980, Vice-President Bush described 'winning' a nuclear exchange as being sure that more than 5 per cent of your own population would survive. Colin Gray, now an adviser to the US National Security Council, said in 1980 'the United States must possess the ability to wage nuclear war rationally.'

Enough of these sickening quotations from those who can talk of the annihilation of millions as if they were dealing in apples and pears. The central problem remains: how to restore a little common sense and how to halt the media's dissemination of right-wing, pro-armament 'defence' policies, which serve only to underpin extremely dangerous ideas about winning nuclear wars.

5   A Twisted Debate

The members of the public are like a flock of sheep: they are easily led. You only have to go on repeating a thing long enough and consistently enough and they will believe it.
Lord Northcliffe

It is sometimes said that there has been a genuine public debate about nuclear weapons in Britain during the last few years. I would like to believe it but I cannot. Having been in the centre of popular nuclear concern for seven years, my impression is that what we have had is not a genuine debate but a propaganda war in which those who hold power in this country have done everything within that power to marginalise, trivialise and defame those who hold views different from their own. All this has been made much easier because the powerful can rely far too often upon a docile media.

Seven years ago I could not have believed that I would ever hold such views. Now, unhappily, I hold them and can easily defend them. The volume of defamation has been amazing.

One of the most scandalous allegations has been that CND is funded by the Soviet Union. It is only a little over a year ago since more than a hundred Conservative Members of Parliament signed an early day motion which claimed that, among other things, CND had received six million pounds from the Soviets in 1981 alone. But as Richard Luce said in 1983, when he was Foreign Office Minister: 'I am aware of no evidence that the USSR has funded CND.' There is none.

CND has not only had to put up with defamation; it has also suffered phone tapping and interference with its mail. It has had spies and informers planted in its office. Individual CND members have been harassed by the Special Branch. Only recently, the office of the Medical Campaign Against Nuclear Weapons was broken into and the membership records were stolen. And when CND has criticised Soviet activity, such as the invasion of Afghanistan and SS20 deployment, the statements are not, or only barely, reported.

The Greenham women have suffered more, as a single group, than any other section of the peace movement. Not only have they been vilified in the crudest personal terms, they have even been accused of harbouring Soviet spies.

Clearly the discussion of issues like security and defence does arouse fierce passion. I am sure that proponents of nuclear disarmament have not always expressed themselves with clinical detachment. Nevertheless, I am certain that the disgusting treatment, by Government spokespeople and semi-Government agencies, of those who hold alternative views about defence and are prepared to argue for them reasonably, would shock the average British voter had he or she any idea of what has gone on in the last few years.

It would be absurd to lay all the blame for what I have called 'a twisted debate' at the door of the media. On many occasions independent sections of the British media have opened up for public view issues which the Government would have much preferred concealed. Three cheers for *Threads* and, at long last, *The War Game*. The history of British nuclear energy accidents and of radiation-linked cancers, both came into the open because of a media independence for which we should be grateful. We should be grateful too for a wide range of informative documentary programmes on radio and television.

But where the media has been really damaging is in the way it has constricted and simplified the nuclear arms debate. It falsely assumes that there are certain parameters within which 'sensible' people operate. Media comment has been dominated by the premise that nuclear weapons 'defend', and that 'balance' in the world of nuclear weapons is somehow important when in fact it is not. The search for parity actually feeds the arms race. The media also regularly accepts the propagandist division of the disarmament movement into 'unilateralists' and 'multilateralists'. That it is perfectly proper to be both and that unilateral steps very often make multilateral agreements possible, is still largely not understood. Yet the United Nations reported in 1984, with only the United States casting a negative vote: 'There is no either/or choice between unilateral and negotiated measures of disarmament. Both are needed in view of their complementary nature.' To deny that states can and should take unilateral or independent steps on the road to disarmament is absurd. The area of intelligent debate should only concern the effectiveness or otherwise of particular independent steps. We would never have reached agreement on the Partial Test Ban Treaty had it not been for President Kennedy's unilateral decision to cease atmospheric testing in 1963.

To a considerable extent the nuclear debate has, over the last few years, been a twisted one. If we could all assume that those who differ from us are not, until proven otherwise, fools or traitors, it might become a more constructive one. Only when the debate has become balanced and the voter properly informed will it be possible to make a rational, considered decision in the polling booth.

6 Labour's Defence Policy: A New Independent Britain

There are only two words to describe [Labour's Defence] document, disingenuous and mendacious.
Ian Davidson, *Financial Times*, December 1986

There is no more glaring example of this twisted debate than the media's response to the Labour Party's defence document, 'The Power to Defend our Country'. Ever since it was published it has been treated with scorn and derision. This is not the kind of treatment handed out to our present Conservative Government which reversed itself on the European Missile Zero Option; moved from gentle criticism to full support of Star Wars; made quite sure that ballistic missiles will not disappear within ten years, as proposed at Reykjavik; ignored the five continents peace proposal; voted against a range of sensible multilateral proposals at the United Nations, including a freeze and a test ban . . .

No. The abuse, from the tabloids through to the heavies, has been aimed with venom at the Labour Party which, unlike the Conservative Party, actually knows there is a problem and is prepared to take some practical steps to solve it.

The problem is the nuclear arms race. Great Britain agreed with 148 other states at the UN in 1978 that 'removing the threat of a world war – a nuclear war – is the most acute and urgent task of the present day.' The Labour Party acknowledges this. The Conservatives, who know only too well how powerful is the appeal of crude nationalism and how easy it is to stir up fears of 'the enemy', do not. And that is why they are a party of nuclear rearmament.

It is particularly odd that Labour's policy should have produced such a howl of media indignation, given that Labour's starting point is military value for money. It cannot be disconnected from the utterances of Mr Schultz, Mr Weinberger, Mr Perle, the American Ambassador and others, all of whom have grossly intervened in British political processes. Independence in Britain is even more dangerous than independence in New Zealand. It is a sign of our new colonial mentality that such Washington intervention passes here almost without negative comment, unlike the response in West Germany where some of Mr Perle's interventions on military matters were recently called by Bonn officials 'irresponsible interference'.

There are two parts to Labour's plan – the first relates to British weapons, the second to American weapons. The case against an independent British nuclear deterrent is a simple one. If the Soviets, who seem forever to be cast as the potential enemies, actually wanted to come here and did not use their nuclear weapons, we would hardly consider launching Polaris missiles knowing that within hours this island would be reduced to cinders. Those who oppose the idea of getting rid of Polaris ought to be willing to answer two questions. Do they ever envisage a time when Britain will not have an 'independent' deterrent and the Superpowers will retain theirs, even at numerically much lower levels? If such a time is to come why not now? If it is not to come then that seems to be a general licence for nuclear proliferation. If Britain is not going to give up its 'independent' deterrent, why should not India be allowed one, or Pakistan, or Iran? The Alliance defence policy seems to suggest that Britain will one day give up its 'independent' deterrent but does not have the courage to specify when. This may be good stuff for those who want to appear to be concerned about disarmament and at the same time play to the current prejudices of some of the electorate, but in reality it is nothing more than an electoral fudge.

The fact is that Polaris, and still less Trident, serves no rational British security purpose, and we in no sense owe it to our allies to keep it going. We did not consult them in advance in 1962 when we decided to purchase Polaris and we did not ask them in 1980 when the Government decided to proceed with Trident. Attlee in 1947 certainly did not consult anyone else when he started us on the nuclear road – he did not even consult all his Cabinet. If the real reason for maintaining an 'independent' deterrent is alleged insurance against threat from some maverick power not yet nuclear, then let us at least be honest enough to say so. It is not the reason now on offer to the electorate.

It is sometimes said that our possession of an 'independent' nuclear system gives us some special leverage when it comes to disarmament negotiations. As a matter of history this is simply not true. By definition we are not present at the bilateral talks between the Superpowers. We have no more influence than anyone else at the forty nation disarmament committee in Geneva, and it could well be argued that at the General Assembly of the United Nations we have actually played a negative role because we have nuclear weapons.

The second part of 'The Power to Defend our Country' relates to American nuclear weapons on our soil – but apparently not the ones on visiting ships. Even so, it is this part that has produced the most indignation. There have been accusations of ingratitude, of sheltering under the American umbrella (how about 'standing under an American lightning conductor'?), and of risking the total withdrawal of American troops from Europe. One day I do indeed hope that American troops will withdraw from Western Europe and Soviet troops from Eastern Europe. Unlike Labour's policy document I do not see a future in which the world seems forever to be divided into the great military blocs. But at the moment it is as much in America's interest to be 'in' Europe as 'in' the Indian Ocean, 'in' the Mediterranean and 'in' the Pacific. America is the global power, it has bases around the world and it plans military pressure wherever its interests are threatened. They are certainly not threatened by the removal from Britain of cruise missiles (which as we all now know arrived for political and not military reasons), F1 11 nuclear bombs and submarine warheads.

The development of the American Trident fleet, with its 6000 mile range, means that submarine facilities are not needed in Scotland to meet the requirements of old-fashioned deterrence. The other two systems, cruise and F1 11s, underpin suicidal flexible response strategies. Labour quite rightly wants to get away from reliance on such insanities. To make it clear that Britain is not prepared to play the flexible response game is a perfectly reasonable way to move NATO as a whole in the same direction.

The 'realist' says he is terrified because the Labour commitment to remove American nuclear weapons from our soil may result in a new isolationism and the removal of the 330,000 American troops in Europe. I am not sure that in the long term that would be the biggest possible disaster. Western Europe, with a larger population, a more effective economy and a much higher technology, is not unable to match the Soviet Union in military terms if it actually had cause to do so. But has it?

The four biggest NATO spenders in terms of GNP are Greece, the United States, the United Kingdom and Turkey. Greece and Turkey are far more concerned about each other than about the Soviet Union. In Britain we have just discovered, not only that American bases and facilities have multiplied quietly, steadily and astonishingly since 1948 but that they can be used not only for NATO purposes but for any purpose that the American military think necessary without any genuine British assent.

On the economic front the picture is not that of a simplistic East–West military confrontation. From Westland to the Nimrod affair we have started to realise that there is a West–West economic war going on. In the Middle East and Central America, American and European interests often collide. The attempted revival of the Western European Union suggests a new concern for European military independence. The recent offer by France of a place under its nuclear umbrella to West Germany makes possible less dependence on the Americans by the Federal Republic.

In short the old bloc positions in the world are already on the move, whether the 'realists' like it or not, and different relationships are in the process of forming. Not all NATO countries have the same defence policies now. Unless we have entirely surrendered national sovereignty there is not the slightest reason why we too should not have an independent position as well.

7   Visions of the Future

*Your sons and your daughters shall prophesy . . . your old men
shall dream dreams, your young men shall see visions.*
Joel 28

'The Power to Defend our Country' is not, to tell the truth, a visionary document. It says nothing about the dreadful poverty of so much of the world, of runaway military budgets, of the hospital closures and welfare cuts which have to be made to balance a budget which includes Trident. It is true that it suggests that a peaceful foreign policy is as important as any rejigging of the military budget in favour of conventional weapons, that common security is more important than individual or bloc security, that nuclear weapons cannot be used to any intelligent end, and so on. But the overriding thrust of the policy is one of cutting Britain's military coat according to her cloth. There is nothing wrong with that, except that security is not only a question of how much can be spent on the means of killing people. Good relations, trust and interdependence are far more important than any increase in conventional military expenditure.

It is smart today to say that organisations like CND, if they were successful, would actually make the world free for conventional war. Lord Carrington went further in an interview in December 1986. 'So many nuclear disarmers seem concerned only with nuclear weapons; they almost seem to suggest that conventional warfare is acceptable . . .'

Acceptable it most certainly is *not*. Those whom he calls nuclear disarmers have actually 'general and complete' disarmament as their final objective. They are convinced that war in any form is not a rational option for humanity. Their concerns are not only nuclear.

But there comes now a point when we have to go beyond the hardware towards a more imaginative way of looking at states and inter-state relationships. It is the 'realists' who, fixed on to national perspectives and over-focused on military solutions, have brought us to the present mess. It is time to take idealism a little more seriously.

The long-term future must mean One World. From the ecological movement, from energy authorities, from civil defence experts, from military assessments like the Palme Report, from the religious groups, and even from the worlds of sport and music the message today is the same. We live in one world, a small finite planet, and we either learn to live together in something like justice and common security or we will destroy ourselves. The threats are plain to see. AIDS, pollution, nuclear war, economic collapse and the like have no respect for national borders. If the people are not to perish then they must have a vision.

One such vision was actually fleshed out in the Charter of the United Nations. Grossly underfunded, crippled by its Security Council Veto, often ignored by the Superpowers who sometimes prefer photogenic bilateralism, the United Nations actually exists. The work of its different agencies has been impressive. Its International Court of Justice has contributed to an understanding of order at a supranational level and its peace-keeping forces have many times prevented open conflict from breaking out. We need to go back to the Charter with a sense of determination. The UN Charter is prefaced by an introduction which talks of saving 'succeeding generations from the scourge of war'. Even the famous Article 51 on 'the inherent right of ... self-defence', which Mrs Thatcher invoked during the Falklands War, made that self-defence conditional. The right to it lasts until the Security Council acts effectively 'to maintain international peace and security'.

It is far too easy to adopt a cynical attitude towards the United Nations. It may be a lifeboat with a number of holes, the greatest of which is ignorance about its function. But it exists and as such, in a destructive world, it is a fragile miracle. What a pleasure it was to see recently an appeal signed by personalities as different as the Archbishop of York and the General Secretary of the Transport and General Workers' Union which stated that, precisely because of all our international problems, 'it is more than ever necessary to support the United Nations'. The aim of the appeal was to raise from governments and peoples the funds needed to make the UN an effective body. Funds alone are not enough. We need a massive programme of education and information about its structure and work. It is ridiculous that sensible educational projects like that of the UN World Disarmament Campaign remain unknown in Britain, because non-governmental groups lack the resources to produce and distribute the posters which ought to go into every school, church, party office and trade union centre.

There is a variety of other institutions which reach out across national borders or at least provide opportunities for discussion on a regional basis. It is a serious and just criticism of the Western Peace organisation that, only late in the day, they are starting to appreciate the potential of the Helsinki process which is rather more than an opportunity for the Americans to thump the Russians over Human Rights. It is a forum for all the countries of Europe to meet to discuss the major issues that divide our continent and to suggest means of healing those divisions. At a lower level, but one of special significance, has been the dialogue between the Government of the GDR and the SPD Party of the Federal Republic on such concerns as chemical warfare and nuclear-free corridors.

We have not only to think about the structure of the United Nations and its charter; it is even more necessary to have some vision about the rule of law, without which we sink into chaos. At the national level we do have a juridical structure, however badly in need it may be of reform. So also do we at the international level, though too often in practice both international law and the world court are ignored.

It is surely also time to rethink our attitude to the conduct of war itself. The military threat is not the greatest danger in the world today. Poverty, unemployment, sickness, loneliness, racial tensions, lack of decent accommodation – these are the real threats to our security. Spend as we like on military preparations, we do nothing comparable to meet these threats.

The budget of the US airforce is larger than the total educational budget of the 1.2 billion children in Africa, Latin America and Asia, excluding Japan. The Soviet Union spends more in one year on military defence than the governments of all the developing countries spend for educational and health care for 3.6 billion people. The world has one soldier for every 200 people, but only one doctor for every 1000. It costs nearly $600,000 a day to operate one aircraft carrier, yet every day 14,000 children die in Africa alone of hunger and hunger-related causes.

This is not a detailed account of the relationship between development and disarmament, although a close examination of the unprincipled commercial pursuit by East and West of the export of weapons shows that relationship to be an exploitative one. It is rather an appeal for indignation. We could do something about the real needs of God's people if we would divert in their direction some of the resources so lavishly used for military purposes. 'Peace,' said Pope Paul VI, 'is the fruit of anxious daily care to see that everyone lives in the justice that God intends.' In the search for justice a little passion is no bad thing. The Bible is not without it.

The Churches are strong on statements condemning the use of nuclear weapons. The Roman Catholic Church in its Vatican II statement 'Gaudium et Spes' of 1965 affirmed that 'any act of war which aims indiscriminately at the destruction of entire cities or wide areas with their inhabitants is a crime against God and Man to be firmly and unhesitatingly condemned.' And the Church of Scotland in 1986 declared that 'no Church can accede to the use of nuclear weapons to defend any cause whatever.' The Church of England Synod in 1983 judged that 'even a small scale first use of nuclear weapons could never be morally justified in view of the high risk that this would lead to full scale nuclear warfare . . .' Unhappily this Synod judgement has not meant that, in practice, the Church of England has faced up to the practical realities of NATO flexible response strategies.

The Churches also give conditional tolerance to nuclear deterrence itself: the theory that by threatening to do something wicked one hopes that one will never have to. It can only be judged '*morally acceptable*' said Pope John Paul in 1982 '*as a step on the way towards progressive disarmament*'. There are few signs that such steps are being taken. On the contrary our Government develops more strategies involving the first use of nuclear weapons, ignores the Soviet 18-month test moratorium, opposes a nuclear freeze on further deployment and does almost nothing to promote such modest initiatives as the United Nations Year of Peace. The Vatican itself in 1985 even suppressed a Pontifical Academy report critical of Star Wars.

The way to peace is an endless painstaking effort to take all the steps which are possible on that road. God has given us the power to act as well as to pray. We could be supporting the United Nations Association and the Campaign Against the Arms Trade. We could get our overseas aid charities to explain that a major cause of poverty is the diversion of resources to 'defence' and war. We could make human contact with the people of the countries supposed to be our enemies. We could have done what governments would not do, and make effective use of the United Nations International Year of Peace. We could make 'human rights' a genuine international concern and not just a weapon in the East–West war. The list is endless and the opportunities are all there. What good sense came from the Dutch Bishops in 1968 when they said: 'Looking for peace means giving peace work a real place, not only as a pious wish in our hearts and on our lips but in our thoughts, in our interests, in our educational work, in our political conviction, in our faith, in our prayers and in our budget.'

From Prime Minister to taxpayer, we all have our personal responsibility for the creation internationally as well as nationally of a climate in which might is not right.

Perhaps all this is too visionary. Perhaps St Paul was also too visionary when he described a unity in which there would

be 'neither Jew nor Gentile, neither slave nor free . . .' Perhaps
Edith Cavell was too visionary when she said, before she died,
'Patriotism is not enough . . .' Perhaps De Chardin was too
visionary when he wrote:

> The age of nations is past.
> The task before us now
> if we would not perish,
> is to build the earth

In this precarious and disjointed present it is difficult to be
too visionary. The realists may tell the visionaries not to rush.
But without the visionaries the realists will have nowhere to
go.

Endpiece

Julia Neuberger

*There would almost certainly be major wars going on in
Europe over the past few decades if we hadn't got nuclear
weapons.*
The Reverend Richard Harries, Bishop-elect of Oxford,
January 1987

The defence and disarmament debate is a curious one. A large
part of it seems to centre on types of weaponry and
equipment. Defence pundits talk knowledgeably about the
effectiveness of certain technologies, even though the honest
doubter often challenges them by saying that proper trials
have not taken place. Those who have earned their glory in
the military field are quite certain of the virtue of defence
strategies, and military scientists produce facts and figures
which seem unchallengeable.

Meanwhile the moral philosophers and religious thinkers
concern themselves with the rectitude of defence policy in
any circumstances. Should one be prepared to kill other
human beings? If so, is such killing only legitimate when it is
soldier to soldier? Is it ever morally defensible to kill
civilians? Is there a 'just war'? If so, how do you define it?
What is the moral legitimacy of developing weapons of mass
destruction? Are weapons which threaten future generations
by their effects, such as radiation, inherently more immoral
than those which do not? Or are all weapons immoral?

Yet those are only parts of the debate. In his essay, Bruce
Kent captures the moral ground on the illegitimacy of nuclear
weapons:

The taking of hostages is not a new idea, but we have
massively increased its scale and called it nuclear
deterrence. It is supposed to have brought peace. Figs do

not grow on thorn bushes. Peace cannot come from terror
and threats of mass murder. . . . The Churches are strong
on statements condemning the use of nuclear weapons.
The Roman Catholic Church in its Vatican II statement
'Gaudium et Spes' of 1965 affirmed that 'any act of war
which aims indiscriminately at the destruction of entire
cities or wide areas with their inhabitants is a crime
against God and Man to be firmly and unhesitatingly
condemned.

Strong stuff, for which echoes are to be found in the Church of
Scotland's statement and even, to a small extent, in a synod
judgement of the Church of England in 1983.

Yet there is sound historical precedent for the just war
doctrine in Christianity. This is documented accurately by
Richard Harries in his recent book *Christianity and War in a
Nuclear Age**, where he argues that 'the just war tradition
exists to insist that morality is applicable to war, as to
everything else in human life.' So some wars would seem to
be defensible, although Bruce Kent would not accept Richard
Harries' thesis that it is legitimate for Christians to stand in
the just war tradition, in which the 'concern is not to
eliminate all possibility of war, which it regards as an
unattainable goal under the conditions of human existence,
but to stop particular wars, which are liable to break out. . . . If
the deployment of nuclear weapons continues to dissuade,
that is, if deterrence is fundamentally stable, then the
criterion of success is more than adequately met.'†

This very different view from that of Bruce Kent is uttered
by a distinguished churchman. It is quoted here because
Bruce Kent's excellently expressed moral arguments are not
tackled on a theological basis by Lord Carver and Lord
Chalfont, although in all other respects the debate is well
matched.

Besides the straight moral argument about nuclear weapons

---

*Mowbrays, 1986.
†Harries, op. cit.

which goes back to the late 1950s and early 1960s (part of which has its roots in the just war debate), there are two other crucial areas on which the debate should initially focus. These are first, the likelihood of accidents, which underlined the attempt to hold non-proliferation treaties and international conferences, and which President Reagan's Strategic Defense Initiative (SDI or 'Star Wars') is supposedly partly about. And secondly there is the issue of whom we should believe about threats to our security. Is it true that the Soviet Union stands ready to pounce, building up its nuclear arsenal so that the West has no chance in the face of Russian greed for world domination? Or is it America which really seeks world domination, with bases in every available area, weapons trained on the Warsaw Pact countries, deeply dependent on a Europe committed to NATO? Do we in Britain need to play any part in the struggle between the Superpowers, or could we just as easily withdraw from the whole defence debate on the basis that we are irrelevant to it and would do better to spend our money on health rather than missiles? Or should we keep our own nuclear deterrent, on the grounds that no one is to be trusted?

These are crucial questions in the debate, yet they are too rarely taken up. Lord Carver, in his cool appraisal of choices available to the public in defence policy, talks of the Liberal–SDP Alliance 'genuflecting in both directions' towards an independent nuclear deterrent on the one hand and a non-nuclear stance on the other, and argues that it 'emphasises the European dimension, playing down the American, although recognising the vital importance of maintaining the latter's support of European defence.' Is that because Britain cannot trust either Superpower? Or is it because the Alliance sees a third great power in the shape of Europe, dependent neither on the USSR nor on the USA, as would seem correct given David Owen's recent speeches?

Lord Carver himself has no hesitation in seeing value in British dependence on and involvement in NATO. Discussing the maintenance of an independent nuclear deterrent in case of American withdrawal from Europe, he says: 'If either

NATO in its present form or such a limited Western European alliance could survive American withdrawal, the importance which we have attached to the American presence – and which I for one still strongly do – would have been shown to be mistaken . . .' Lord Chalfont is even stronger on this issue, seeing a moral virtue on the American side and a real threat, almost an evil, on the Soviet side: '. . . it is possible to assert as a general principle that Russian military strength is entirely disproportionate to any possible requirement for the territorial defence of the Soviet Union . . .' 'In the case of an obsessively secret totalitarian power, with no free press and no opposition', as he claims, it could be argued that it is impossible to arrive at the exact intentions of the government concerned, although Lord Chalfont asserts the evidence of some defectors from the Soviet Union who 'have provided persuasive, if not entirely conclusive, evidence of the existence of a grand design for global predominance.' He also quotes from The Penkovsky Papers on the differences in quality of mind and techniques of reasoning between an American or an English general on the one hand and a Soviet general on the other, were they handed a set of 'objective facts and scientific data, with instructions that these facts and data must be accepted as impeccable, and an analysis made and conclusions drawn on the basis of them . . .' The author of The Penkovsky Papers is quite sure that 'the Soviet general would arrive at conclusions which would be radically different from the other two. . . . a different set of moral laws governs and restricts the behaviour of the Soviet.'

Lord Chalfont by no means shares the extreme views on the nature of the Russians caricatured by Bruce Kent in his contribution. He starts his section 'The Soviet Threat' with a quotation from Michael Heseltine in 1983: 'The problem is very clear. We are dealing with a monolithic Soviet power. That's the real enemy. That's where the real threat is.' Bruce Kent writes: 'In these few words Michael Heseltine did indeed make very clear where the real risk is. It is in his mind and in the minds of thousands like him, in positions of great power in Britain. It lies in the conviction that, monolithic, inexorable, ruthless, the Soviet Union is forever the enemy that waits to attack us.' Bruce Kent's analysis is partly a Socialist one; he sees the Soviet Union as being perceived as a threat by the West 'because it challenged fundamental positions about property and social control.' But it is also an analysis based on accurate observation of the lack of success by the Soviets in their foreign policy. He quotes the failure to maintain a brotherly relationship with China as the most notable example, but adds the loss of influence in Yugoslavia, Indonesia, Egypt, Algeria, Ghana, Iraq and Sudan, while arguing that 'Romania shows a greater independence from its Soviet superpower partner than any NATO country from the US.' That is, of course, arguably true at present, but the history of 'independent' Warsaw Pact countries has not necessarily been a happy one, as Hungary, Czechoslovakia and Poland have demonstrated. The true parallel should perhaps be American involvement with foreign countries, where its policy has been to destabilise Socialist powers, such as Allende in Chile, and to replace them with governments sympathetic to US interests.

Bruce Kent does not attempt to analyse in detail why it is 'that the Soviet Union so easily becomes seen as the evil enemy at the door ...' That, he states, is 'a matter for educationalists and psychologists as well as politicians. In part it was no accident. Anti-Sovietism has played a profound part in British thinking for many years.' And he quotes George Kennan, US ex-Ambassador to the Soviet Union, as saying: 'The image of a Stalinist Russia, poised and yearning to attack the West ... was largely the creation of the Western imagination'.

Yet Lord Carver, who plainly does not share the picture of the Soviet Union as the evil force 'poised to attack the West', argues that involvement in NATO is crucial to our well-being, including as it does the threat of the use of nuclear weapons, even though he feels that President Reagan has confused the issue both by SDI and at Reykjavik. For until that point, with 'the President's vision' of 'rendering these nuclear weapons impotent and obsolete' being sprung on his unsuspecting allies, 'the latter had rested content to shelter under a nuclear umbrella, the mainstay of which was a belief in the strategic stability of a situation in which the two great Superpowers maintained a capability of wiping each other out.' Bruce Kent would reject this position as quite immoral, but Lord Carver is undoubtedly correct in his analysis of what America's allies had really been thinking. The situation – however immoral, in Bruce Kent's terms of the building up of nuclear arsenals – was stable, in that both sides believed that neither would be willing to wipe the other out for fear of what would happen to themselves. 'As long as that was the case, the risks to both of allowing their forces to engage in direct conflict with each other, and the presence of the forces of both on either side of the Iron Curtain, appeared to be a stable guarantee that the status quo in Europe would be preserved.'

But SDI has changed all that. Lord Carver points out that the views that any present or future British government has on the US Strategic Defense Initiative 'are not likely to have any significant influence on the programme one way or another'. He argues correctly that all this will be determined by American domestic politics and the relationship between the Superpowers. He says, tongue in cheek perhaps, that 'if all the European members of NATO were united in their views, they might exert a marginal influence'. And he continues: 'Most of them, including our own government, had misgivings about it from the start; but none of them wants to miss an opportunity to jump on the technology bandwagon.' A very sober approach, particularly as he concludes: 'Any future British government would be wise to maintain a cautious non-committal attitude, and wait and see how the programme develops.'

Less sober by far, but illustrative of the nature of the debate about SDI in Britain, was an article by Simon Hoggart* which began: 'If the whole idea of Star Wars isn't the most tremendous fraud, then the argument about it is. President Reagan has been busily selling it to the world on the grounds

*Observer, 11 January 1987.

that it could protect mankind forever from the horrors of nuclear war. The President has always had a taste for science fiction and happy endings, and that's how he's managed to drum up his support . . .'

What is Star Wars about? In popular imagination it has come to be an impenetrable shield, so that Soviet missiles would be destroyed before reaching the US. The reality, however, is quite different. SDI is not an attempt to stop all Russian missiles hitting US targets, since many are bound to get through, but 'to make the first strike so difficult and so risky that the Soviets decide that it simply isn't worth while'. It would work by various weapons, including lasers, trying to hit Soviet weapons as they rise from the earth, or during their journey towards their destinations, or as they drop down on to their targets. Given that so many weapons would not get through but would be destroyed en route, the Russians would need far more warheads – up to a million, according to Dr Allan Mense, chief scientist for SDI – to have the same effect. The argument is that SDI does not need to be a totally protective shield; rather, it needs to so threaten the plans of the enemy that they no longer seem worth carrying out.

Lord Chalfont reminds us that 'there has been a tendency to ignore the work which the Soviet Union is doing in this field', for the Soviet Union has been conducting research in the laser field and others. Chalfont admits that 'the United States is undeniably well ahead in some aspects of space-based defence research and certainly has the potential to widen the gap between it and the Soviet Union'. Yet 'there is little doubt that in some areas the Soviet Union itself is well advanced.' Nevertheless, Lord Chalfont argues that the Soviet Union is not yet in the American league in this area, 'and the intensive Soviet campaign against the Strategic Defense Initiative almost certainly arises from a fear that the scientific and economic resources of the United States would enable the Americans to overtake the Russian effort and to deploy effective strategic defence systems long before the Soviet Union could do so.' Hence, Lord Chalfont argues, the Russian insistence at Reykjavik 'that the United States should abandon its research into space-based ballistic missile defence systems (SDI)', which the Americans, understandably, refused to do.

But this is not how it appeared to everybody. Lord Carver argues that Reykjavik

> has not only resurrected all the previous arguments on the issue, but has provided a far more radical background against which NATO, and Britain in particular, has to make decisions about nuclear weapons policy. Had it not been for Mr Gorbachev's insistence on setting strict limits on research into space-based antiballistic missile systems and President Reagan's refusal to accept them, both were apparently prepared to agree to a 50 per cent cut in strategic nuclear delivery systems, to the abolition of either *all* ballistic missiles (the US proposal) or all strategic delivery systems (the Soviet proposal), and to the withdrawal of all intermediate-range delivery systems west of the Urals . . .

As Lord Carver comments with devastating accuracy: 'The possibility that the two Superpowers might have agreed on such far-reaching reductions rang alarm bells in Europe. It looked like decoupling with a vengeance.' ('Decoupling' refers to the weakening of the threat that a Warsaw Pact invasion of Western Europe could escalate to a strategic nuclear strike against the Soviet Union; it was seen as undermining the general nuclear deterrent to war, making it likely that if a war broke out and led to a nuclear exchange, such an exchange would be limited to Europe west of Russia; and that, short of war, it would lead to 'nuclear blackmail', in other words make it possible for the Soviet Union to intimidate the countries of Western Europe into adopting policies favourable to itself, as Hitler had done, by the threat of war if they refused.) Decoupling is a peculiarly European concern, particularly of the Federal Republic of Germany. It was concern with decoupling that caused the doubts about Reykjavik long before the talks came to grief, even though the projected reductions in arms pleased many of the European

'Greens' as well as the disarmers worldwide.

Many European governments see a stability in the status quo and want no significant reductions on account of the decoupling threat. Against that has to be set the objections of those 'who saw a proliferation in the numbers of nuclear weapons and an increasing danger both of conflict itself and of its leading to the nuclear devastation of the Continent.' This is one of the central arguments of the entire debate. Does proliferation of nuclear weapons render the world even more unstable? Do arms limitation treaties have any validity? Is there any advantage in the Superpowers alone having nuclear weapons? Or is there a role for an independent British, or European, nuclear deterrent?

Indeed, one of the key questions to be asked is whether arms control really is necessary. Conference succeeds conference on arms control, and, as Professor Michael Howard* put it, 'Diplomats take the path to Geneva which their fathers took in the 1950s and their grandfathers in the 1930s; as they go through the traditional wrangles about stock-piles and comparability and verification which are almost as time-honoured as the rituals of the Roman Catholic Church . . .' Is any greater security to be gained from negotiating away some of the massive stockpiles of weapons? Bruce Kent would plainly think there is, since in his terms a reduction would be better than nothing. This would be partly because of the reduction in the risk of accidents, since he, unlike many others, believes that there is major risk:

> There are those . . . who believe that a war involving the use of nuclear weapons cannot happen because technical arrangements make that impossible. . . . If you believe that you are crossing the road on a high wire rather than on the pavement you will have a different understanding of risks.

> If a nuclear war by accident is not a possibility then it is not clear, since there is no point in deliberately

---

*'Is Arms Control Really Necessary?', lecture given on 8 October 1985.

starting one, why there should be any urgent need to reduce nuclear stockpiles. For instance, President Reagan correctly stated in February 1986: 'We want agreements that truly diminish the nuclear danger.' I am sure he is quite sincere. But what is the danger if deterrence is a secure system?

This is undoubtedly a question worth asking. If deterrence is a secure system, why have there been the 1963 Partial Test Ban Treaty, the 1967 Outer Space Treaty, the 1968 Non-Proliferation Treaty, the 1972 Anti-Ballistic Missile Treaty, the 1972 Strategic Arms Limitation Talks (SALT I) Agreement, not to mention SALT II, as well as the Conference on Disarmament in Geneva, the Mutual (and Balanced) Force Reduction talks in Vienna, the Conference on Confidence and Security Building Measures and Disarmament in Europe, held in Stockholm, as well as the bilateral US–Soviet 'umbrella' talks in Geneva? Clearly there is a sense among even the most seasoned and hardened soldiers that there is some point in holding these discussions, that reduction of stockpiles has an inherent value (either reduction of risk or cost), and that perhaps discussions themselves make war more difficult to start. Michael Howard* asks the question which we all need to ask: 'Is the whole arms-control industry in fact the modern equivalent of the alchemist's search for a philosopher's stone which will turn the lead of international tensions into the gold of perpetual peace?'

Bruce Kent would say that it is, and that arms control is not the issue, but disarming. He reminds us that we live in 'a world obsessed with military security. . . . In the long term there can be no absolute security. "Remember that you are dust and to dust you shall return" . . . Security cannot be bought.'

Oddly enough, few serious thinkers would dispute that, and certainly neither Lord Carver nor Lord Chalfont would do so. What they would say, however, is that whilst absolute

---

*op. cit.

security is unobtainable, relative security is available; and skilful negotiation and sensible handling of the nuclear issue, as well as general defence policy, can assist in providing that security. Lord Carver states very firmly: 'The overall deterrent to war in Europe, represented by the combination of the presence of the forces of the two Superpowers on either side of the Iron Curtain and the fact that they both have the capability to inflict terrible damage on each other, strongly reinforces the deterrent which forces on the ground, backed by air and naval forces, represent . . .' The deterrent brings 'security' in itself, whilst the fact of negotiation and balance makes the deterrent 'equal'. Lord Chalfont salutes the 'real and genuine concerns' of those who exert pressure for arms control and disarmament. He argues: 'Effective defence policies must therefore go hand in hand with the pursuit of balanced, multilateral and verifiable arms control agreements. In this context it is important to recognise that it is *war* which we seek to avoid, not just nuclear war.' There is security in deterrence and in balanced reductions. Yet Lord Chalfont argues that 'the evidence of history is that arms races alone do not cause wars. The causes of war are subtle and intricate . . .' That is undeniably true, but the risk of nuclear accident is there and the larger the stockpile the greater it is, whilst the Chernobyl disaster illustrates how terrible a nuclear disaster can be even when it is nothing to do with weapons.

All three authors devote a part of their papers to conventional weapons. Lord Chalfont, having argued that 'it is war which we wish to prevent, not just nuclear war', quotes General Rogers (Supreme Allied Commander Europe) as insisting that 'even with adequate conventional capabilities, NATO could never be certain of defeating a conventional attack without escalation', which suggests a strong reliance on the nuclear deterrent. Yet he also argues hard for an improved strength of British 'contribution to the conventional defence of Western Europe', and he continues: 'In due course it should be possible to redeploy to Europe the military resources at present committed to non-NATO tasks in Northern Ireland, the South Atlantic and Hong Kong.'

It is Lord Carver, however, who examines the question of conventional forces in detail. He argues hard against short-term political remedies: 'As a professional soldier . . . I cannot but express my dismay at the way in which the real defence choices become submerged under the instant remedies which the politicians, the media, and those who profit from both, expound.' He argues that 'nuclear weapons cannot be relied on as a substitute for conventional forces' and that therefore those conventional forces 'should be adequate to fulfil their task, which is primarily to prevent war by ensuring that a potential opponent should not think that he could gain a potential advantage by the use of armed force.' Lord Carver does not feel that NATO has to match 'man for man, tank for tank, aircraft for aircraft' all the forces which the Warsaw Pact could theoretically mobilise. But he does feel that they must be related to the forces the Warsaw Pact could mobilise at short notice and that their equipment should be adequate, arguing that at present it is either 'already qualitatively inferior to that of the Soviet armed forces or will soon become so.'

He then examines the various options. Since many people believe Britain cannot afford to make a significant contribution both to NATO's maritime forces and to its land and air forces in Europe, the common view is that we must choose between the two. The majority of military experts and commentators go for strengthening the Navy – since, more than any other NATO nation with the possible exception of Norway, we are vulnerable to attack within the sea and from it. Yet Lord Carver, in the light of his experience, does not regard the option of reducing the army as a sensible one. 'The fact remains that, for a country of 56 million people, we produce a very small army.' He does not believe that there is a real choice between navy and army. 'Geography, determining our history, forces us to make a delicate judgement on the balance between the maritime and the continental commitment. We cannot give one priority over the other.'

He then analyses the present position and concludes that there is little justification for a vastly increased maritime fleet, but that there is a strong argument for serious spending on some of the new technology which increases 'the effectiveness of fire-power without increasing the demands on manpower . . . It offers the possibility of much more accurate and immediate detection of potential targets by sources which, apart from airborne early warning, do not rely on manned aircraft.' Lord Carver argues that these systems are expensive but that 'if they replace the aircraft on which NATO has hitherto relied for the same reconnaissance and strike tasks, nuclear and conventional, and if battlefield nuclear systems are abolished, they should not cost more (perhaps less) than replacement of those systems . . .' Apart from that, Lord Carver argues that the new systems are not viciously offensive in nature, as sometimes portrayed, and would not provoke particular fears in Warsaw Pact countries. 'In reality they consist merely of replacing concepts based on aircraft, relying heavily on the delivery of nuclear bombs, with missiles delivering either solely non-nuclear warheads or, at least, relying much less than previously on early use of nuclear ones.' This may be a stretched definition of conventional forces, but it is to Lord Carver's credit that his analysis of available weapons and strategies is so detailed and that he clearly favours non-nuclear advanced technology in this instance.

Bruce Kent, however, disapproves of conventional weapons almost as much as nuclear ones. 'The ultimate aim has to be a world free from the weapons of mass destruction.' But he sees the arena of the conventional weapons debate as providing 'room for more uncertainty and probably more propaganda'. He is dubious about the picture regularly presented of a NATO 'ever vulnerable to overwhelming Soviet conventional forces', and finds it strange that the picture is presented in this way when the NATO countries 'have twice the population of their Warsaw Pact counterparts and many times the economic strength.' He quotes George Younger as claiming that we now face 'a huge overwhelming preponderance of conventional weapons', and contrasts this remark with the *Military Balance* annual review published by the International Institute for Strategic Studies which said that 'the conventional military balance is still such as to make military aggression a highly risky undertaking for either side.' And, although he is plainly delighted by the unilateralist policy Labour has taken on nuclear weapons, he seems less than satisfied with the rest of Labour's defence document. It 'is not, to tell the truth, a visionary document. . . . It is true that it suggests that a peaceful foreign policy is as important as any rejigging of the military budget in favour of conventional weapons . . .' But all in all, it does not excite him, except in anger at the way it has been vilified so generally by the media.

But before examining the party policies, we are still left with some questions. Lord Chalfont suggests that 'the geo-political and economic centre of gravity is beginning to shift from the European–Atlantic area to the Pacific basin.' He goes on to say that this is partly responsible for the increasing American impatience with the European allies. That there is impatience is without doubt true: American journalists and political commentators make that clear enough. But to what extent this is due to difficulties in NATO or to the fact that Europe is no longer perceived as central, is unclear. If the global picture remains the American Superpower on one hand and the Russian on the other, there is no doubt that Europe is still crucial as the battleground between the two. If the picture is seriously one of 'a global threat to the free world', and the dangers are perceived in the Warsaw Pact and elsewhere – Central America, for instance – then Europe may be less important in that struggle. But part of the reason may be economic. As the United States sees a more united Europe and a European monetary system less dependent on the dollar than sterling has been, the sphere of influence is clearly reduced and America needs to look for markets elsewhere. The result of that is a switching of interest – both economic and defence – to those new markets. Europe, for so long the buffer zone between the two Superpowers, may gradually cease to be so. And that could clearly have profound influence on NATO, even eventually leading to a question the Americans will need to ask themselves, as to whether NATO is worth maintaining and funding. Both Lord Chalfont and Lord Carver see Britain as within the American sphere of influence, and involved in NATO, for the long term. Bruce Kent, for moral reasons, does not. There may be entirely different arguments from the American side that have not yet been fully aired, which make NATO an organisation to be scrapped as being of limited or dubious value, expensive, and protecting an area that the United States feels less concerned with than it has done.

This situation is made more complicated by the position of France within NATO, since it is not a member of the Eurogroup. (The Eurogroup was set up within NATO in 1968 and all other alliance European members are members of it.) France also has its own independent nuclear deterrent, as Britain does at present. Both Britain and France are Permanent Members of the United Nations Security Council, and both own a range of nuclear weapons of various types. The argument has been that, should the NATO alliance disintegrate, there would still be two national European forces which might deter nuclear attack by threatening severe retaliatory damage on the USSR. The Soviet Union has therefore argued that both British and French strategic forces should be taken into account in arms control agreements between East and West. It maintained that French and British ballistic missile submarines are part of the Western strategic capability and that therefore any increase would give the Soviet Union the right to a corresponding increase in her submarine-based forces. The USSR, at this point, also called for the question of the status of British and French forces to be resolved. But the United States refused. In the Intermediate Nuclear Forces (INF) negotiations, when the Soviet Union tried to count British and French forces against Soviet SS20 land-based missiles, the United States, in agreement with its NATO allies, rejected the claim, arguing that SS20s were more comparable with Pershing II and cruise missiles. The debate continues, and how long the non-negotiability of British and French forces can be maintained is an open question.

Nevertheless, both governments remain reluctant to 'trade in' their forces, presumably because they fear that their minimum deterrents would be cut to below credibility level.

This would suggest that there might be some virtue in greater cooperation between Britain and France on nuclear delivery systems. David Owen of the SDP rearticulated this long-standing argument in May 1985, and since then there have been several suggestions, mostly from the SDP, of greater Anglo-French and greater European cooperation in this area. The report of the Joint Liberal–SDP Alliance Commission on Defence and Disarmament, published in June 1986 and much publicised since as proof of disagreements between the two parties, is quite clear on this point: 'The members of the European Community should now be ready to go further and develop common policies, in order both to carry more weight in international affairs than they can individually and to increase the effectiveness of their defence spending by common research, development and procurement of equipment. . . . We want to see a marked change in the balance of decision making in NATO between the US and the European members . . .'

Lord Carver does not entirely agree, although sympathetic to some of this thinking. And on the crucial issue of an independent nuclear deterrent, he has this to say: 'I would, if necessary, be prepared to let the French be the only European nation to waste its money on independent nuclear weapon systems.' He argues this through a strong commitment to NATO, but the political parties divide differently in Britain, and significantly so.

Labour has just published, at the time of writing, its defence document 'The Power to Defend our Country'. It argues for 'military value for money', and goes for unilateral nuclear disarmament, echoing the detailed defence policy document of 1984: 'Labour believes that Polaris should be phased out in successful arms negotiations in the next few years. If this is not done, Labour will, on assuming office, decommission Polaris from service.' Trident would also be cancelled. Labour would also seek the removal of American cruise missiles from British soil, as well as F1 11 nuclear bombs and submarine warheads. It would, however, increase spending on conventional forces, specifically in strengthening the conventional force contribution to NATO, by laying emphasis on the Navy. Nor does Labour pledge itself to withdraw from NATO, although the reaction from NATO's other members to the radical non-nuclear line is not clear. And in a recent exchange of letters with George Younger, Secretary of State for Defence, Mr Kinnock wrote that the only way out of the 'nuclear dilemma' was to combine strengthened conventional forces with a NATO policy of 'No first use' of nuclear weapons.

The Liberal–SDP Alliance meanwhile has had its difficulties, particularly over the issue of an independent deterrent. Whilst committed to scrapping the Trident programme, they agreed finally to maintaining 'our minimum deterrent until it can be negotiated away as part of a global arms negotiation process, in return for worthwhile concessions by the Soviet Union which would enhance British and European security.' And, in modernising that deterrent, it would be 'frozen at a level no greater than that of the Polaris system'. It would be assigned to NATO; it would not be an independent strategic system. The Alliance also argues for increased European activity independent of the United States, and for improvements in conventional forces, to be paid for by savings made from reductions in forces maintained outside NATO, such as in the Falkland Islands.

The Conservatives would press ahead with the Trident programme. The new programme is for Trident D5, a much more sophisticated and accurate system than the old C4, as a successor to Polaris. Trident D5 allows a greater number of targets than Polaris and Chevaline, and gives Britain the second-strike capability for going to the heart of Soviet government targets which the Conservatives believe necessary.

All the political parties argue hard for increased arms control negotiation. Labour clearly believes that this is for disarmament purposes. The Alliance and the Conservatives are less sure. Such negotiation may have more to do with verification, balance, reductions in particular capabilities and areas, and keeping the channels of communication open than with true disarmament. But they share a stated aim of peace and security, and all share a commitment to NATO, although the nature of that commitment varies.

Only the present Conservative Government asserts the non-negotiability of Britain's nuclear deterrent. Both Labour and the Alliance support the principle of immediate inclusion of British (and French) forces in arms control negotiations, although Labour's position seems to give the Soviet Union a political incentive to making concessions rather than a strategic one, since British nuclear weapons are to be scrapped whatever the Soviet response is.

The question remains open as to whom Britain should trust. Is it the United States, or the rest of Europe, or Europe within NATO? Should we view the world as divided into great Superpower military blocs? Is the Soviet Union the dangerous enemy some perceive it to be? Where does Britain's best interest lie in this vexed and oversimplified issue of defence and disarmament?

Bruce Kent, Lord Carver and Lord Chalfont challenge some of the tacit assumptions and put forward strong views, but perhaps the last word should remain with Professor Michael Howard;* who argues, though far from sure himself, that political considerations demand that 'Governments must be seen to be striving to attain the Heavenly City of disarmament: even if the goal is unattainable, the object is a noble one, and the very process of trying to reach it will be a civilising and pacifying influence on international behaviour.'

---

*op. cit.